By Roman Hands

Inscriptions and Graffiti for Students of Latin

Second Edition

By Roman Hands

Inscriptions and Graffiti for Students of Latin

Second Edition

Matthew Hartnett

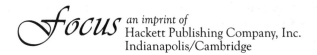 an imprint of
Hackett Publishing Company, Inc.
Indianapolis/Cambridge

By Roman Hands

© 2012 Matthew Hartnett

Previously published by Focus Publishing/R. Pullins Company

Focus an imprint of
Hackett Publishing Company, Inc.
P.O. Box 44937
Indianapolis, Indiana 46244-0937

www.hackettpublishing.com

ISBN 13: 978-1-58510-402-4

Printed in the United States of America.

20 19 18 17 16   3 4 5 6 7 8

The paper used in this publication meets the minimum requirements of American National Standard for Information Sciences—Permanence of Paper for Printed Library Materials, ANSI Z39.48–1984.

∞

Table of Contents

Grammatical Table of Contents

Thematic Table of Contents

Preface to the First Edition

The aim of this book is to provide students and teachers with a collection of Roman inscriptions and graffiti that illustrate basic elements of Latin grammar and syntax and, at the same time, illuminate interesting and important aspects of Roman history and culture. *By Roman Hands* is built on three premises: First, students do not need to wait until the third year of high school or the second year of college study to grapple with authentic Latin. If the texts are well chosen and equipped with running vocabulary and suitable notes, students are not only capable of comprehending them, but will advance more quickly to legitimate facility with the language by being exposed to real Latin early on. Second, inscriptions and graffiti provide brief, clear and self-contained examples of good Latin in actual use, and serve as vivid introductions to fascinating aspects of Roman history, life and thought. Third, a student who is given the opportunity to hone his translation skills on examples of Latin left by actual Roman hands will be excited by the directness of his engagement with the ancient world and will find his study of Latin more enjoyable and rewarding as a result.

Latin teachers regularly intone that learning the language well is the key to understanding the Romans. But students at the early levels, who test their mettle against passages of artificial Latin for the most part, and who quickly come to associate forays into history and culture with taking a break from their Latin, have reason to doubt whether their labors are getting them any closer to the Romans. A student will, however, truly appreciate the value of her efforts when mastery of a grammar lesson affords her direct access to an actual moment in Roman time—when knowing the difference between the ablatives of means and personal agent enables her to see what killed a gladiator from Dacia (**37**); when construing an ablative absolute correctly means appreciating how skillfully Octavian could turn civil war into propaganda (**100**); when properly identifying a condition opens a window into the mind of a frustrated traveler desperate to see his beloved (**159**).

While the constraints of class period and semester never make it easy to incorporate more material into the curriculum, any exercise that simultaneously combines reinforcement of grammar, exposure to authentic Latin and insight into Roman culture surely merits comparison with any competing use of time. This book can be used in a number of ways: as a reservoir of examples for reinforcing grammar points as they are introduced; as a supplement to the translation exercises in the regular textbook; as a source of additional assignments for more able or energetic students; as a tool to aid students in preparing for periodic major exams; or as a comprehensive review of basic grammar and syntax for students who are about to embark on the translation of extended passages of Latin literature for the first time.

To facilitate ease of use within the parameters of class time, the inscriptions have on the whole been kept on the shorter side, either by selection or by the careful excerption of brief sense units from longer texts. Each inscription is represented first in a form that approximates the appearance of the lettering on the original object, and then in an edited version that will be more familiar and accessible to students. The goal here is to permit students to see Latin as it was actually written by the Romans, without demanding of them the specialized skills of a trained epigrapher. If exposure to these inscriptions sparks an interest in pursuing epigraphy further, that can only be counted a benefit, and the *Suggestions for Further Reading* will provide curious students with wonderful places to continue their investigation.

Each selection is followed by a brief commentary that elucidates cultural and historical matters germane to the interpretation of the text, draws attention to noteworthy features of language or thought, and orients the student to the context of the message being conveyed. This is followed by a running vocabulary of all but the most common or easily intuited words, combined with notes that explain obscure grammar and offer translation help where needed. The vocabulary and notes offer more support in Parts 1 and 2 to assist the student just embarking on the study of Latin, and gradually less in Parts 3 and 4, when knowledge of the preceding grammar and syntax is assumed, along with a wider familiarity with the most commonly used Latin words. At the back of the book there is a comprehensive vocabulary that glosses every word used in the inscriptions, along with a grammatical index that cites every inscription illustrating a given grammar point. Many of the texts are illustrated by photos or line drawings of the originals. For teachers who prefer to access the inscriptions by theme, a *Thematic Table of Contents* is provided in addition to the *Grammatical Table of Contents*. In addition, thematic cross-references in the commentary assist students in comparing inscriptional evidence and drawing broader conclusions about the nature of Roman history, life and thought.

Thanks are due to the donors of the Barlow Chair and the Loudon Fund at St. Mark's School and to the staffs of the Widener Library at Harvard University, the Clapp Library at Wellesley College, and the St. Mark's School Library. I wish to extend my deep appreciation to David Conti, Ed DeHoratius, George Franko, Richard Geckle and James Kothe for reading and commenting on earlier drafts of this work. I must also acknowledge my debt to Torey Akers for her excellent line drawings and to Helen Pope of St. Stephen's School in Rome, as well as Michael O'Donnell, for photographs of several inscriptions *in situ* in Rome. They have helped make this a much better book than it might otherwise have been. Finally, thanks to my family for graciously allowing me the time and space to complete this project.

Preface to the Second Edition

The aims and scope of By Roman Hands remain essentially unchanged with the second edition. However, those familiar with the earlier edition will notice several differences. Most significantly, the book has been expanded by the inclusion of 26 additional texts and nine new illustrations. Of these new texts, 13 are shorter ones scattered throughout Parts 1 through 4, six fall into a new section on imperatives, and seven are longer readings that together constitute a new *Part 5: Additional Inscriptions for Practice and Review*. The order of the inscriptions has also been modified to accord with the grammar presentation of Susan Shelmerdine's very sound *Introduction to Latin*, although the order of topics does not in fact differ much from the first edition, nor indeed from that found in most introductory textbooks. Finally, the notes have been lightly revised with an eye toward offering students just the right level of support—neither too little nor too much—as they advance toward fluency in the language.

I must extend my thanks to Ron Pullins of Focus Publishing for his support of this project from the beginning and for his encouragement to revise the book for a second edition; to the users and reviewers of the first edition for their thoughts and suggestions; to Steve Lewis and Paul Langford for help with illustrations; and to the faculty of the Department of Classical Languages at Phillips Exeter Academy for their collegiality, advice and support.

Matthew Hartnett
Exeter, NH

Introduction

The Study of Roman Inscriptions

The study of inscriptions (called "epigraphy," from the Greek word for inscription) provides students of ancient Rome with an incomparable source of information about Roman life, both public and private. It has been estimated that over 300,000 Latin inscriptions have been found. Some of these can still be seen in the place (*in situ*) where the Romans put them, others have been removed from their original locations and can be seen in museums, still others were seen and recorded at some time between antiquity and the present, but have since been lost. Those inscriptions that remain, which must be a small percentage of the total number produced by the Romans, nevertheless convey an indelible impression of the duration and geographical extent of Roman civilization. Inscriptions have been found all across the Roman Empire, from the British Isles to the Persian Gulf, from North Africa to the Black Sea. And these inscriptions range in time from at least the fifth century BC to the fifth century AD and beyond.

In the middle of the nineteenth century, a group of German scholars conceived of the ambitious project of researching, recording and cataloguing all known Latin inscriptions and publishing them in one place. The title of this imposing multi-volume collection is *Corpus Inscriptionum Latinarum*—usually referred to by the abbreviation *CIL*. Work on this impressive collection, which currently boasts 17 volumes, many of which are themselves comprised of numerous volumes and additional supplements, continues to this day. In addition, many other smaller collections have appeared over the years which facilitate access to the most interesting and important of the hundreds of thousands of texts included in *CIL*. However, the standard means for citing a Latin inscription is still according to its location in *CIL*, thus the entry for each inscription in this book cites, whenever possible, its location in *CIL* by volume and inscription number (e.g., *CIL* 10.6942). In addition, references are provided to several useful collections of inscriptions published in English whenever an inscription included here appears also in that collection (e.g., Gordon 50). The full titles of all the works thus cited can be found in the *Abbreviations of Collections of Inscriptions*.

Types of Roman Inscriptions

The term inscription refers to a variety of different types of texts that were written, scratched, painted or incised on a variety of materials, including stone, marble, metal, and clay, and for a variety of purposes, ranging from public commemoration to personal insult. The inscriptions represented in this book can be categorized conveniently as follows:

- **Building inscriptions**. These inscriptions record the construction, or sometimes reconstruction, of temples, arches and other public works. They often record the person or group responsible for the work, as well as any individual to whom the work might be dedicated. See, for example, the inscriptions from the Arch of Titus (**16**) and the Temple of Isis (**145**).

- **Honorific inscriptions**. These inscriptions, often found on statue bases, honor the life and achievements of a particular individual. See, for example, the inscriptions in honor of Julius Caesar (**68**) and Lucius Valerius Pudens (**162**).

- **Dedicatory inscriptions**. These inscriptions are found on altars or other objects consecrated to the gods. In their simplest form, they record nothing more than the name of the god or gods in the dative case. See, for example, the altar dedicated to Minerva and Hercules (**17**). Others might include details of the achievements of the dedicator. See, for example, the dedication by Lucius Mummius (**102**).

- **Epitaphs**. These inscriptions are found on gravestones, marble slabs, the walls of collective tombs, cinerary urns, or the wall niches designed to hold them. The simplest of these give the name of the deceased, the duration of the deceased's life, and the name(s) of the individual(s) responsible for the monument (**107**). In other cases, one may find the life and character of the deceased described in great detail (**139**) or ruminations on the nature of life and death (**41**).

- **Inscriptions on portable objects**. These are inscriptions found on smaller objects made of metal or clay or other materials. See, for example, the inscriptions found on a ring (**9**), a plate (**63**), a clay lamp (**122**), and a slave's collar tag (**55**).

- **Graffiti and dipinti**. This category encompasses all of the texts and drawings scratched (graffiti) or painted (dipinti) on walls and other surfaces. Dipinti typically include election endorsements (**153**) and announcements of gladiatorial shows (**19**). Graffiti are casual and unofficial scrawls that can touch on just about any topic, ranging from wishes of happiness (**126**) to threats against rivals (**158**).

It should be noted that many of the inscriptions collected in this book fall into more than one category. For example, the inscription on the Arch of Titus (**16**) is both a building inscription and an honorific text. It should also be noted that the selections from the Vindolanda tablets (see **134**, **141**), along with the ancient Roman lullaby (**48**), are properly categorized neither as inscriptions nor graffiti, but belong to the discipline of Classics known as "paleography" (from the Greek for "old writing"). Because of their great interest, however, these texts have been included here and, for convenience, suggestions for further reading on the Vindolanda tablets are included under the heading "Inscriptions and Graffiti."

The Language of Roman Inscriptions

The style of Latin used in Roman inscriptions varies widely. At one end of the spectrum, there are the official inscriptions found on public buildings and other monuments, which, aside from being more compressed and elliptical than the Latin of Cicero or Ovid, generally adhere to the rules of grammar and syntax that we associate with "Classical Latin." At the other end of the spectrum, there are the graffiti and epitaphs written by private individuals, which often exhibit peculiarities of spelling, grammar and syntax that depart from the standards found in literary authors. To a large extent, these differences are a function of education and social class. The language used by Roman authors is the product of a tradition of formal composition and studied expression that was generally accessible only to the upper classes. But the vast majority of the Latin-speaking inhabitants of the Roman world spoke and wrote (if they could write) a less uniform and ever-evolving form of Latin known as "Vulgar" Latin. The term is a misleading one. Although many of the graffiti from Pompeii could aptly be described as vulgar in the ordinary sense, the word "vulgar" (from *vulgaris, -e*, "of the common people") in this context means "common" or "everyday," with the implication that it is characteristic of the lower classes. It is this Latin, or, more precisely, these various forms of Latin, that gradually morphed, during the centuries following the collapse of the Roman Empire, into the Romance languages that are spoken today: Italian, French, Spanish, Portuguese and Romanian.

Whenever a peculiarity of spelling or usage occurs in the inscriptions collected in this book, the standard classical equivalent is supplied either in the text itself or in the notes that follow each entry. Some typical peculiarities are these: substitution of vowels (e.g., **sepe** instead of **saepe**; **monimentum** instead of **monumentum**); confusion of double consonants (e.g. **puelarum** instead of **puellarum**; **promitit** instead of **promittit**); the omission of **m** at the end of a word (e.g., **maximu** instead of **maximum**); ablative of place where without a preposition (e.g., **caelo** instead of **in caelo**); ablative of duration of time, as opposed to accusative (e.g., **vixit annis II** instead of **vixit annos II**). For a detailed discussion of these and other features of Vulgar Latin, see the *Suggestions for Further Reading*, under "The Latin Language," and also Wallace, *An Introduction to Wall Inscriptions from Pompeii and Herculaneum*, pp. xxiv-xxxvii.

Many of the texts included here are composed in poetic meter—that is to say, the words are arranged in such a way that the alternation of long and short syllables and the number of syllables in each line follow a certain recognizable pattern. Since most students are not taught poetic meter until after they have learned the basic grammar and syntax of the language, metrical issues are not addressed in this book. Students and teachers who wish to explore this dimension of the texts will find several helpful commentaries in the *Suggestions for Further Reading*.

Reading Roman Inscriptions

To a student looking at a Latin inscription on stone for the first time, the text can appear both familiar and strange. The letters are usually instantly recognizable, but they are all capitals, and they are arranged in a way very different from the conventions of most Latin textbooks. Words are not always separated by spaces, words carry over from one line to the next with no hyphenation, and there is no punctuation aside from the occasional dots ("interpuncts") that float at mid-line between words (e.g., DE · SVO · FECIT). In addition, as might be expected of a text inscribed on the surface of a hard stone of limited size, words are frequently abbreviated to the point of obscurity (e.g., F for FILIVS). On top of that, the Romans would regularly leave out words when they could easily be inferred from the context. On the other hand, something as seemingly straightforward as a name could sometimes require dozens of words to express. In inscription **100**, for example, the identification of Octavian takes up twelve out of the seventeen words on the stone.

The lettering of an inscription can range from the exquisitely regular and carefully executed forms of the Column of Trajan (**163**) to the cruder and less uniform letters found on the dedication by Lucius Mummius (**102**). Even in the latter case, however, the letters are clearly formed and precisely distinguished from one another. We should not forget, moreover, that the Romans often colored in the letters of an inscription with red paint, making them stand out with much greater contrast than their present colorless outlines would suggest. In addition, monumental inscriptions often featured bronze letters that were either attached to the smooth surface of the stone or fitted into carved letter-shaped recesses. If one looks carefully at the inscription on the Arch of Titus (**16**), for example, one can see the small holes that facilitated the attachment of the original bronze letters, now lost.

Roman graffiti, on the other hand, which are, in effect, examples of Roman "cursive" writing, exhibit a much wider range of possibilities. While the letters in the Labyrinth graffito (**2**) roughly approximate the forms familiar from inscriptions on stone, many of the letter forms in "Poor Wall" (**88**) depart considerably from that norm, and the lettering of, say, "In Praise of Love" (**119**), is all but indecipherable to anyone but an expert. Line drawings and photographs of these and other examples are included in this collection so that students may begin to appreciate what goes into deciphering and interpreting these ancient texts and also, very simply, so that they may see what Latin *looked like* when written, scratched or incised by actual Roman hands.

Epigraphic Conventions Used in This Book

All inscriptions, whether they were incised on stone or some other object, or painted on a surface such as a wall, are printed here in boldface type. Each inscription appears twice.

Transcription

In the **transcription**, the inscription as it appears on the stone or object is represented as accurately as possible, including layout and division into lines, e.g.,

T{H}ELYPHVS SAMNES

NATIONE TRAEX

Note that Roman inscriptions are executed in capital letters with no punctuation, although they often employed spaces or interpuncts (·) between words. Note also that "V" was used to represent both "v" and "u." Two types of symbols may appear in the transcription. Braces { } indicate extra letters or letters included by the engraver by mistake. These letters are not printed as part of the **text** (see below). Second, square brackets [ ] indicate letters lost or illegible on the original object, but restored by a scholar's conjecture. These letters are printed as part of the **text** (see below).

Text

In the **text**, the same inscription is represented, but with upper and lower case letters, standard punctuation, abbreviations filled out, "u" and "v" distinguished, and unusual or archaic spellings regularized, e.g.,

Telyphus, Samn*is*, natione T<h>*rax*.

Two types of symbols may appear in the **text**. Angular brackets < > indicate letters omitted by the engraver but added by a modern editor. Parentheses ( ) indicate letters that are added by a modern editor to expand an abbreviation. Long vowels are marked by macrons only in forms of the first declension and the word *hic, haec, hoc* that would otherwise be ambiguous, and in the infinitive form of 2nd conjugation verbs. Finally, the use of italics indicates a regularization of an unusual or archaic spelling. This is the only non-standard epigraphic convention used in this book.

Summary of Epigraphic Conventions Used in this Book

[ABC]   letters lost or illegible, but restored by a scholar's conjecture

<abc>   letters omitted by the engraver, but added by a modern editor

{ABC}   extra letters or letters included by the engraver by mistake

(abc)   expansion of an abbreviation

abc   unusual or archaic spelling that has been regularized

Abbreviations of Collections of Inscriptions

CIL	*Corpus Inscriptionum Latinarum*
Courtney	E. Courtney, *Musa Lapidaria. A Selection of Latin Verse Inscriptions*
Gordon	Arthur E. Gordon, *Illustrated Introduction to Latin Epigraphy*
ICUR	*Inscriptiones Christianae Urbis Romae*, nova series
Keppie	Lawrence Keppie, *Understanding Roman Inscriptions*
RIB	*The Roman Inscriptions of Britain*
TAB VIND	*The Vindolanda Writing Tablets*
Wallace	Rex E. Wallace, *An Introduction to Wall Inscriptions from Pompeii and Herculaneum*

Abbreviations of Grammatical Terms

abl.	ablative
acc.	accusative
act.	active
adj.	adjective
adv.	adverb
c.	common
compar.	comparative
conj.	conjunction
dat.	dative
decl.	declension
dir. obj.	direct object
f.	feminine
fem.	feminine
fut.	future
gen.	genitive
imperat.	imperative
imperf.	imperfect
indic.	indicative
infin.	infinitive
m.	masculine
masc.	masculine
n.	neuter
neut.	neuter
nom.	nominative
partic.	participle
pass.	passive
perf.	perfect
pers.	person
pres.	present
plur.	plural
sing.	singular
subj.	subject
subjunct.	subjunctive
transl.	translate/translation
voc.	vocative

PART 1

Nouns: The Uses of the Cases

I. Nominative and Accusative

1. S.P.Q.R. (*CIL* 10.6942)

SENATVS

POPVLVSQVE

ROMANVS

Senatus populusque Romanus.

Inscription found at Capua in Italy. A frequently used and often abbreviated formulation designating the government of Rome, beginning in the Republican period and continuing through the Empire. Revived in the modern period, S.P.Q.R. can be seen on modern public buildings and manhole covers in the city of Rome today.

> **populusque**: **-que** is a suffix meaning "and," to be translated before the word to which it is attached.

2. Labyrinth (*CIL* 4.2331)

LABYRINTHVS
HIC · HABITAT
MINOTAVRVS

Labyrinthus. Hīc habitat Minotaurus.

A graffito from Pompeii. The myth of Theseus and the Minotaur was apparently popular in Pompeii. In addition to the crude representation above, several wall paintings and a mosaic have been found depicting the tale. These can now be seen in the National Archaeological Museum in Naples.

> **labyrinthus**: a title, as it were, for the drawing.
> **hīc**: "here." To be distinguished from **hic** (short i), meaning "this" or "this man."
> **habitat**: habito, -are, -avi, -atum, *to live, dwell.*

3. Waiting (*CIL* 12.5193, 3)

VIRVM · ECXPECTO · MEVM

Virum exspecto meum.

From a gravestone found at Narbo (Narbonne, France). As in many Roman epitaphs, the deceased is to be understood as speaking the words. What conception of the afterlife is implied by this sentiment?

> **virum**: vir, viri, m., *man, husband.*
> **exspecto**: exspecto, -are, *to wait for.* The italicized *s* indicates the regularization of an unusual or unclassical spelling.
> **meum**: meus, -a, -um, *my, mine.*

4. Love is (Almost) Everywhere (*CIL* 4.7086=Wallace II.138; *CIL* 4.111; 3117)

a.

MARCVS SPEDVSA AMAT

Marcus Spe<n>dusa<m> amat.

b.

MARCELLVM
FORTVNATA · CVPIT

Marcellum Fortunata cupit.

c.

SERENA
ISIDORV
FASTIDIT

Serena Isidoru<m> fastidit.

Three graffiti from Pompeii.

Marcus: Marcus, -i, m., *Marcus*.

Spe<n>dusa<m>: Spendusa, -ae, f., *Spendusa*. Angular brackets indicate a letter omitted by the person who scratched or engraved the text, but added by a modern editor.

Marcellum: Marcellus, -i, m., *Marcellus*.

Fortunata: Fortunata, -ae, f., *Fortunata*.

cupit: cupio, cupere, *to desire, want*.

Serena: Serena, -ae, f., *Serena*.

Isidoru<m>: Isidorus, -i, m., *Isidorus*.

fastidit: fastidio, -ire, *to despise*.

5. Deceiver (*CIL* 4.5251; Wallace II.135)

RESTITVTVS MVLTAS DECEPIT
SEPE PVELLAS

Restitutus multas decepit s*ae*pe puellas.

A graffito from Pompeii. In view of the many romantic encounters described
on the walls of Pompeii, it is not surprising to find an accusation of infidelity.
Another graffito (**52**) reports that a Vibius Restitutus spent the night alone at
an inn longing for his girlfriend, but it is uncertain whether it is the same man.

>   **Restitutus**: Restitutus, -i, m., *Restitutus*.
>   **decepit**: "has deceived."

6. Magic Square (*RIB* 2.4.2447.20; Keppie, pp. 123-4)

R O T A S
O P E R A
T E N E T
A R E P O
S A T O R

Rotas operā tenet Arepo sator.

Found scratched into a wall in the Roman city of Corinium (Cirencester,
England). This arrangement of letters can be read forward, backward, up
and down to yield the same words. Examples of this particular version have
also been found in Italy, Portugal, Syria and Hungary. The sense of the whole
seems to have been less significant than the arrangement itself, although it may
have conveyed some special meaning for the Christians with whom it became
associated. Many imaginative but unconvincing reconstructions of its hidden
symbolism have been attempted.

>   **rotas**: rota, -ae, f., *wheel.*
>   **operā**: "with care" (abl. sing. of opera, -ae, f., *effort, care*).
>   **Arepo**: a proper name otherwise unattested, probably invented to make
>   the square work.
>   **sator**: sator, -oris, m., *sower, planter; father.*

7. Proof of Divinity? (*CIL* 6.29609, 5-6)

**CINIS · SVM · CINIS · TERRA · EST · TERRA · DEA · EST ·
ERGO · EGO · MORTVVA · NON · SVM ·**

Cinis sum, cinis terra est, terra dea est, ergo ego mort*u*a non sum.

From an epitaph found on the *Via Latina* in Italy, in which the deceased presents an argument for her own immortality. How convincing is this argument?

> **cinis**: cinis, cineris, m., *ashes, ash.*
> **sum**: "I am."
> **est**: "is."
> **dea**: dea, -ae, f., *goddess.*
> **ergo**: adv., *therefore.*
> **mort*u*a**: mortuus, -a, -um, *dead.*

8. Here Lies Helpidius (*CIL* 6.9241, 2-4)

**HIC · IACET · HELPIDIVS · FATIS
EXTINCTVS · INIQVIS · EGREGIVS · IVVENIS
CAVSARVM · ORATOR · HONESTVS**

**Hīc iacet Helpidius, fatis ex*s*tinctus iniquis,
egregius iuvenis, causarum orator honestus.**

Epitaph of the orator Helpidius, otherwise unknown, found in Rome. In these lines, the moral goodness of the young man is contrasted with the iniquity of his death. For "unjust fates," see also **57**.

> **iacet**: iaceo, iacēre, *to lie, lie dead, repose.*
> **Helpidius**: Helpidius, -i, m., *Helpidius.*
> **fatis iniquis**: "by adverse fates."
> **ex*s*tinctus**: "having been killed," masc. nom. sing.
> **egregius**: egregius, -a, -um, *excellent, outstanding.*
> **iuvenis**: nom. sing. of iuvenis, iuvenis, c., *young man, young woman.*
> **honestus**: honestus, -a, -um, *honorable, respectable, distinguished.*

9. Pledge of Love (*CIL* 12.5693, 8)

BONAM   AMO TE

VITAM   AMA ME

SERVA FIDEM

Bonam vitam! Amo te. Ama me. Serva fidem.

Inscribed on a ring found at Aquae Sextiae (Aix-en-Provence, France). The use of rings as tokens of love is well attested in Roman culture. See, for example, Plautus, *Miles Gloriosus*, Act IV and Ovid, *Amores* II.15.

> **bonam vitam**: accusative of exclamation.
> **te**: acc. sing. of tu, *you*.
> **ama**: imperat. sing. of amo, amare, *to love*.
> **me**: acc. sing. of ego, *I*: "me."
> **serva**: imperat. sing. of servo, servare, *to keep, preserve, maintain*.
> **fidem**: acc. sing. of fides, fidei, f., *faith, faithfulness*.

10. Bed and Breakfast (*CIL* 13.2031, 1-4)

MERCVRIVS HIC LVCRVM

PROMITIT APOLLO SALVTEM

SEPTVMANVS HOSPITIVM

CVM PRANDIO

Mercurius hīc lucrum promit\<t\>it, Apollo salutem,
Septumanus hospitium cum prandio.

From Lugdunum (Lyon, France), now lost. Presumably it was originally posted as a sign above the door of an inn run by Septumanus. The rest of the inscription reads, "Whoever comes here will find himself better off afterwards; traveller—watch out where you stay!" What does this inscription imply about the number of inns available at Lugdunum? Find Lugdunum on a map of ancient Gaul. Why should it come as no surprise if there were many inns located here? For other inscriptions relating to inns, see **52**, **54**, and **61**.

> **Mercurius**: Mercurius, -i, m., *Mercury*.
> **lucrum**: lucrum, -i, n., *profit*.
> **promit\<t\>it**: promitto, -mittere, *to promise*.
> **Apollo**: Apollo, Apollinis, m., *Apollo*.
> **salutem**: acc. sing. of salus, salutis, f., *health*.
> **Septumanus**: Septumanus, -i, m., *Septumanus*.
> **hospitium**: hospitium, -i, n., *hospitality; an inn, lodging*.
> **cum prandio**: "with lunch."

11. Vergil, Adapted (*CIL* 4.9131; Courtney 60; Wallace II.159)

FVLLONES VLVLAMQVE CANO NON ARMA VIRVMQ

Fullones ululamque cano, non arma virumq(ue).

A graffito found on a clothes cleaner's shop in Pompeii. For reasons that are not entirely clear, these establishments were associated with the owl (*ulula*). In this case, the "author" adapts the familiar opening of Vergil's *Aeneid*, "arma virumque cano…" to incorporate a reference to launderers and owls.

fullones: fullo, fullonis, m., *a launderer*.
ululam: ulula, -ae, f., *owl*.
cano: cano, canere, *I sing*.
arma: arma, armorum, n., *weapons, arms*.
virumq(ue): the parentheses indicate expansion of an abbreviation.

12. Trinity (*CIL* 3.3247, 2-5)

TERRA TE
NET CORPVS NO
MEN LAPIS ATQVE
ANIMAM AER

Terra tenet corpus, nomen lapis atque animam aer.

From an epitaph found at Tibiscum (western Romania). What view of death is implied by this sentiment?

corpus: acc. sing. of corpus, -oris, n., *body*.
nomen: acc. sing. of nomen, nominis, n., *name*.
lapis: nom. sing. of lapis, lapidis, m., *stone*.
animam: anima, -ae, f., *spirit, soul*.
aer: nom. sing. of aer, aeris, m., *air, the air*.

13. The Good Life (*CIL* 6.15258, 5-8; Courtney 170a)

BALNEA · VINA · VENVS
CORRVMPVNT · CORPORA
NOSTRA · SET · VITAM · FACIVNT
B · V · V

Balnea, vina, Venus corrumpunt corpora nostra,
se*d* vitam faciunt b(alnea) v(ina) V(enus).

From an epitaph inscribed on a marble tablet found in Rome. From the rest of the inscription, we know that this marked the grave of Tiberius Claudius Secundus, freedman of the emperor Claudius. Despite (or perhaps due to) his love of the good life, Secundus lived to the age of 52—a relatively long time by ancient Roman standards. In the inscription above, notice that there is no "and" joining *balnea*, *vina*, and *Venus*. The omission of conjunctions like this is known as "asyndeton." What effect does it have here?

> **balnea**: balnea, balneorum, n., *baths, the baths.*
> **vina**: vinum, -i, n., *wine.*
> **Venus**: Venus, Veneris, f., the goddess *Venus.* Here, the word Venus
> is used to mean "love" or "sexual love." When one word is used
> as a substitute for another word with which it is associated
> (e.g., "Washington" for "the U.S. government"), this is called
> "metonymy."
> **corrumpunt**: corrumpo, -rumpere, *to weaken, destroy.*
> **nostra**: noster, nostra, nostrum, *our.*
> **faciunt**: facio, facere, *to make, do.*

14. A Toddler's Brief Life (*CIL* 6.35957)

NYMFIS · SVBITA
NEA · MORTE · NE
CATVS · VIXIT · BRE
VE · TEMPVS · AN ·
· V · M · VI · D · VIII

Nymfi<u>s subitaneā morte necatus, vixit breve
tempus an(nos) V, m(enses) VI, d(ies) VIII.

Inscribed on a small marble sarcophagus found at Narnia (Narni, Italy). The death of a boy so young (and by some external agent, as the use of *necatus* implies) is made more poignant by the fact that his brief life is measured out to the day.

Nymfi<u>s: Nymfius, -i, m., *Nymfius.*
subitaneā morte: "by a sudden death."
necatus: "having been killed," masc. nom. sing.
vixit: "lived."
d(ies): acc. plur. of dies, diei, m., *day.*

15. To Our Stephanus (*CIL* 6.22102, 7)

O FATVM INFELICEM QVI TE N[OBIS ABSTVLIT]

O fatum infelicem, qui te nobis abstulit.

From an epitaph inscribed on a broken tablet found in Rome, in which the departed Stephanus is addressed by his grieving wife Moschis.

fatum: fatus, -i, m., *fate.* Variant of the more common fatum, -i, n.
infelicem: masc. acc. sing. of infelix, infelicis, *unlucky, woeful; unhappy, miserable.*
qui: "which," referring to **fatum** and subject of **abstulit**.
te: acc. sing. of tu, *you.*
nobis: "from us." The square brackets indicate letters lost or illegible on the original object, but restored by a modern editor.
abstulit: "carried off," "stole."

II.   Genitive and Dative

16. Arch of Titus (*CIL* 6.945; Gordon 50; Keppie, pp. 45-6)

SENATVS
POPVLVSQVE · ROMANVS
DIVO · TITO · DIVI · VESPASIANI · F
VESPASIANO · AVGVSTO

Senatus populusque Romanus divo Tito divi
Vespasiani f(ilio) Vespasiano Augusto.

Inscription on the southeast side of the Arch of Titus in the Roman Forum.
Located on the *Via Sacra*, the route taken by generals celebrating military
triumphs, the arch itself depicts in sculpted relief the triumph of Titus following
his sack of Jerusalem in AD 70. Since the inscription refers to "the deified" (*divus*)
Titus, it must have been erected sometime after his death in AD 81. As often in
dedicatory inscriptions (e.g., **17**), the verb is omitted. Understand "dedicated
this arch" with the subject *senatus populusque Romanus* and indirect object
divo Tito Vespasiano Augusto.

divo: divus, -a, -um,
    divine; deified.
**Tito…Vespasiano
    Augusto**: Titus
    Vespasianus
    Augustus, known
    as Titus, emperor
    AD 79-81.
Vespasiani: Titus
    Flavius
    Vespasianus,
    known as
    Vespasian,
    emperor
    AD 69-79.

17. Dedicatory Altar (*CIL* 7.313; *RIB* 1200)

**DEAE ME
NERVAE
ET
HERCVLI
VICTOR[I]**

Deae Minervae et Herculi Victori.

An altar found near the site of a Roman fort called Epiacum (now known as Whitley Castle) in Northumberland, England. As with **16**, the verb is omitted. What words can be supplied to make sense of the datives?

    Minervae: Minerva, -ae, f., *Minerva*.
    Herculi: dat. sing. of Hercules, -is, m., *Hercules*.
    Victori: dat. sing. of victor, victoris, m., *conquerer, victor* (here, an epithet of Hercules).

18. The End (*CIL* 6.20674b, 1-2; Courtney 174)

**IAM · DATVS · EST · FINIS · VITAE · IAM
PAVS{S}A · MALORV M**

Iam datus est finis vitae, iam pausa malorum.

From an epitaph inscribed on a large marble urn found in Rome, now lost.
What view of life is implied by this sentiment? What view of death?

> **datus est**: "has been given," "there has been given."
> **finis**: nom. sing. of finis, finis, m., *end.*
> **pausa**: pausa, pausae, f., *pause, end.* Braces indicate extra letters or letters
> included by the engraver by mistake.

19. Gladiator Show (*CIL* 4.1189; Wallace I.60)

**A · S{S}VETTI{I} · CER[T]I
AEDILIS · FAMILIA · GLADIATORIA · PVGNABIT
POMPEIS · PR · K · IVNIAS · VENATIO · ET VELA ·
ERVNT**

**A(uli) Suetti Certi aedilis familia gladiatoria
pugnabit Pompeis pr(idie) K(alendas Iunias.
Venatio et vela erunt. A(uli) Suetti Certi aedilis
familia gladiatoria pugnab(it) Pompeis pr(idie)
K(alendas) Iunias. Venatio et vela erunt.**

A dipinto (painted text) found at Pompeii, announcing a gladiatorial show. Many other gladiatorial announcements have been found in the city, including others advertising this very show. These announcements typically give the name of the individual responsible for organizing and funding the show, the date, the type of fighting that can be expected, and any additional attractions that might be of interest to the audience. One can deduce from the mention of *vela* ("awnings") here, along with references elsewhere to sprinkled water, that it could grow uncomfortably hot in the seating area of the amphitheatre.

A(uli) Suetti Certi: *Aulus Suettius Certus.*

aedilis: gen. sing. of aedilis, aedilis, m., *aedile*, an elected position in Roman government responsible for, among other things, the administration of games.

familia: familia, -ae, *family, household* (including slaves), but also, as here, group.

Pompeis: locative of Pompei, -orum, m., *Pompeii:* "at Pompeii".

pr(idie) K(alendas) Iunias: "the day before the Kalends of June", or May 31st.

venatio: nom. sing. of venatio, -onis, f., *an animal hunt.*

vela: velum, -i, n., *sail,* or, as here, *awning.*

20. Heartthrob (*CIL* 4.4289; Wallace II.66)

PVELARVM
DECVS CELADVS

Puel<l>arum decus Celadus.

A graffito found at Pompeii. We know from other graffiti that Celadus was a gladiator who fought as a Thracian (*Thrax*), that is, with a helmet, greaves, round shield, and short sword or dagger. This is one of several graffiti that allude to his popularity with young women. For other gladiators, see **36**, **37**, and **58**.

decus: nom. sing. of decus, decoris, n., *glory.*

Celadus: Celadus, -i, m., *Celadus.*

21. No Loitering (*CIL* 4.813; Courtney 157; Wallace I.96)

OTIOSIS · LOCVS ·   HIC NON EST DISCEDE
MORATOR

Otiosis locus hic non est. Discede, morator.

A dipinto (painted text) found at Pompeii, next to an image of a snake. The snake represents what was known to the Romans as the *genius loci*, the protective spirit of a place, which this text warns potential loiterers from profaning. See also **120**.

> **otiosis**: otiosus, -a, -um, *idle, at leisure.* In Latin, as in English (e.g., "the good, the bad, and the ugly"), an adjective may be used in place of a noun. Here, the adjective **otiosis**, because it is masculine plural, may be translated "idle men" or "loiterers."
> **hic**: masc. nom. sing. of hic, haec, hoc: "this."
> **discede**: imperat. sing. of discedo, -cedere, *to leave, depart.*
> **morator**: voc. sing. of morator, -oris, m., *delayer, loiterer.*

22. To Jupiter (*CIL* 8.18219, 1-6)

IOVI OPTIMO MA
XIMO DEORVM PRINCIPI
GVBERNATORI OM
NIVM RERVM
CAELI TERRARVM
QVE RECTORI

Iovi Optimo Maximo, deorum principi, gubernatori
omnium rerum, caeli terrarumque rectori.

From a dedicatory inscription found at the legionary camp at Lambaesis (Algeria). The collection of epithets attached to Jupiter's name here leave no room for doubt as to the extent of the god's power, both in the heavens and on earth.

> **Iovi**: dat. sing. of Iuppiter, Iovis, m., *Jupiter.*
> **Optimo Maximo**: "Best and Greatest," a frequent epithet of Jupiter.
> **principi**: dat. sing. of princeps, principis, m., *leader, chief, prince.*
> **gubernatori**: dat. sing. of gubernator, -oris, m., *steerer, governor.*
> **omnium**: fem. gen. plur. of omnis, omne, *all, every.*
> **rerum**: gen. plur. of res, rei, f., *thing, matter, affair.*
> **rectori**: dat. sing. of rector, -oris, m., *director, ruler.*

23. Talented Woman (*CIL* 3.10501, 3; Courtney 115)

VOX EI GRATA FVIT PVLSABAT POLLICE CORDAS

Vox ei grata fuit, pulsabat pollice c<h>ordas.

From a sarcophagus found at Aquincum (Budapest, Hungary). The rest of the inscription records that Titus Aelius Iustus, an organ-player attached to a legion of the Roman army, commissioned it for his wife, Sabina, a woman "cultivated in the arts, who, alone, excelled her husband." On women and the arts, see **66**.

> **vox**: nom. sing. of vox, vocis, f., *voice.*
> **ei**: fem. dat. sing. of is, ea, id, *he, she, it.* Translate: the voice "to her," or "her" voice.
> **grata**: gratus, -a, -um, *pleasing.*
> **fuit**: "was."
> **pulsabat**: pulso, pulsare, *to beat, strike, pluck.*
> **pollice**: "with her thumb."
> **c<h>ordas**: chorda, -ae, f., *string* (of an instrument).

24. Too Soon (*CIL* 6.20128, 4)

QVID MIHI TAM SVBITO MAXIMVS ERIPITVR

Quid mihi tam subito Maximus eripitur?

From an epitaph inscribed on a marble tablet, now in the Vatican Museum. An example of a "rhetorical question," a question that is asked not to elicit an actual response, but to generate some effect. What is the effect of the rhetorical question here?

> **quid**: "why?"
> **mihi**: dat. sing. of ego, mei, *I.*
> **Maximus**: Maximus, -i, m., *Maximus.*
> **eripitur**: "is being snatched away."

25. A Good Citizen (*CIL* 7.1166; *RIB* 289)

**BONO REI
PVBLICAE
NAT**

Bono rei publicae nat(us).

Inscribed on a statue base found in Wroxeter, England. The statue, if there was one, did not survive with its base.

> **rei publicae**: gen. sing. of res publica: "of the republic." Alternatively, a dative of reference.
> **nat(us)**: "born," masc. nom. sing.

26. Mother and Daughter (*ICUR* 2.4233, 8)

SOLACIO MATRI TV QVOQVE MATER ERAS

Solacio matri tu quoque Mater eras.

From a grave inscription known from a manuscript at the Vatican. See also **116** and **87**. The line contains a play on the word *mater*: the deceased, a girl named "Mater," is described as being a comfort to her own *mater*. The words above are addressed to the deceased.

> **solacio**: solacium, -i, n., *solace, comfort*.
> **tu**: nom. sing. of tu, *you*.

27. Busy Work (*ICUR* 4.12416)

**LABORA ASELLE QVOMODO EGO LABORAVI
ET PRODERIT TIBI**

Labora, aselle, quomodo ego laboravi, et proderit tibi.

A graffito found in a schoolroom on the Palatine Hill in Rome. Presumably a sarcastic aside by a bored student who inventively compares his schoolwork to the seemingly endless (and pointless, as far as the ass is concerned) turning of a mill.

LABORA ASE ILE QVOMODOEGOLABORAVI
EIPRODERIITIBI

aselle: asellus, -i, m., ass, *donkey*.
quomodo: adv., *how*.
laboravi: "I have worked."
proderit: 3rd pers. sing. fut. of prosum, prodesse (+ dat.): "it will benefit."
tibi: dat. sing. of tu, *you*.

28. Plea for Divine Help (*CIL* 4.2310k; Wallace II.153))

TV · DEA TV PRESE NOSTRO SVCCVRRE LABORE

Tu, dea, tu pr<a>ese<ns>, nostro succurre labori.

A Graffito from Pompeii which quotes Vergil, Aeneid 9.404.

tu: nom. sing. of tu, *you*.
pr<a>ese<ns>: praesens, -entis, *present; propitious*.
nostro: noster, -tra,-trum, *our*.
succurre: succurro, -ere, *help, run to help*.
labori: labor, -oris, m., *work, labor; distress, suffering*.

29. To Statilia Hilara (*CIL* 6.6250, 5)

TV · NOSTRI · MEMENTO · NOS · NVMQVAM ·
OBLIVISCEMVR · TVI

Tu nostri memento; nos numquam obliviscemur tui.

From an epitaph found in Rome. From the rest of the inscription, we learn that Statilia Hilara was a freedwoman and that her husband was the chief steward of a household (*atriensis*) as well as a painter (*colorator*). The words above are addressed to the deceased.

    tu: nom. sing. of tu, *you.*
    nostri: gen. plur. of ego, *I.*
    memento: imperat. sing. of memini: "remember."
    nos: nom. plur. of ego, *I.*
    obliviscemur: "we will forget."

30. Nothing to Fear in Death (*CIL* 5.8974, 5-6)

NIL · MALI · EST
VBI · NIL · EST

Nil mali est, ubi nil est.

From an epitaph found at Aquileia in Italy. What view of death is implied by this sentiment?

    nil: nihil.

III.   Ablative

31. Oldest Profession (*CIL* 4.1948; Wallace II.122))

LVCILLA EX CORPORE LVCRVM FACIEBAT

Lucilla ex corpore lucrum faciebat.

A graffito from Pompeii..

Lucilla: Lucilla, -ae, f., *Lucilla*
corpore: abl. sing. of corpus, -oris, n., *body.*
lucrum: lucrum, -i, n., *profit.*
faciebat: facio, -ere, *to make, do.*

32. Busy Staphylus (*CIL* 4.4087; 2060; Wallace II.123)

a.

STAPHILVS HIC CVM QVI[ETA]

Staphilus hīc cum Quietā.

b.

ROMVLA
HIC · CVM
STAPHYLO
MORATVR

Romula hīc cum Staphylo moratur.

Two graffiti from Pompeii. The name "Quieta" can be confidently restored on the basis of other graffiti in which this woman's name appears. Note that the name "Staphylus" is spelled differently in each graffito.

moratur: "lingers," "stays."

33. Riot (*CIL* 4.1293; Wallace II.54)

CAMPANI VICTORIA VNA
CVMNVCERINIS PERISTIS

Campani, victoriā una cum Nucerinis peri*i*stis.

A graffito found at Pompeii, which refers to the riot that erupted among spectators in the amphitheatre at Pompeii in AD 59. The event, described by the historian Tacitus (*Annales* XIV.17), made a significant impact on life in Pompeii, as the Roman Senate ordered the amphitheatre closed for ten years as a result. The meaning of the graffito above is probably that the *Campani*, though they defeated the *Nucerini* in the fighting, "perished" also in the sense that they were subsequently deprived of the pleasure of attending gladiatorial shows.

Campani: voc. plur. of Campanus, -a, -um, *inhabitant of Campania, Campanian*. Campania is the region of Italy that encompasses Pompeii, but the term **Campani** here may refer to the members of a particular fan club.

victoriā: victoria, -ae, f., *victory*. Translate: "in victory" (ablative of attendant circumstance).

una: "together" (to be taken closely with **cum**).

Nucerinis: Nucerinus, -a, -um, *inhabitant of Nuceria, Nucerian*. Nuceria is a town in Campania, not far from Pompeii.

peri*i*stis: "you (pl.) perished."

34. Temple of Saturn (*CIL* 6.937)

SENATVS · POPVLVSQVE· ROMANVS
INCENDIO · CONSVMPTVM · RESTITVIT

**Senatus populusque Romanus
incendio consumptum restituit.**

Inscription from the architrave of the Temple of Saturn in the Roman Forum. Originally built in 498 BC, the temple was rebuilt in 42 BC and restored again in the fourth century AD—the restoration to which the inscription refers. The Temple of Saturn served as the state treasury of Rome from the time of the early republic, a use possibly associated with Saturn's role as god of agriculture.

> **incendio**: incendium, -i, n., *fire, conflagration*.
> **consumptum**: "having been consumed" (modifies the unexpressed "this temple").
> **restituit**: "restored" (understand "this temple" as direct object).

35. Priscilla (*CIL* 8.13110, 2-3)

EXIMIA · SPECIE · IACET · HIC · PRISCILLA
PVELLA

Eximiā specie iacet hīc Priscilla puella.

From an epitaph found at Carthage (Tunis, Tunisia). In what other case in Latin could *eximiā specie* be written, with no change of meaning?

   eximiā: eximius, -a, -um, *exceptional, distinguished.*
   specie: abl. sing. of species, -ei, f., *appearance, beauty.*
   Priscilla: Priscilla, -ae, f., *Priscilla.*

36. A Gladiator from Thrace (*CIL* 6.10187)

T{H}ELYPHVS SAMNES
NATIONE TRAEX

Telyphus, Samn*is*, natione T<h>r*ax*.

An epitaph found in Rome. The Samnite was a type of gladiator who fought with the large oblong shield, visored helmet and sword characteristic of the Samnites, a tribe from the mountains of south-central Italy. For other gladiators, see **20**, **37** and **58**.

   Telyphus: Telyphus, -i, m., *Telyphus.*
   Samn*is*: Samnis, -itis, *Samnite.*
   natione: abl. sing. of natio, nationis, m., *birth, nationality.*
   T<h>r*ax*: Thrax, Thracis, *Thracian.* Here, an inhabitant of Thrace, not
      the gladiatorial type "Thracian" (see **20**).

37. A Gladiator from Dacia (*CIL* 3.14644)

AMABILI · SECVTORI
NAT · DACVS · PVG · XIII
FATO DECEPTVS ·
NON · AB HOMINE ·

Amabili secutori. Nat(ione) Dacus, pug(navit) XIII,
fato deceptus, non ab homine.

Inscription found on a cinerary urn near Epetium (Stobrez, Croatia). The *secutor* was a gladiatorial type who wore a helmet and carried a large curved oval or rectangular shield, along with a short sword or knife. The *secutor* (literally, "pursuer") possibly derives his name from the pursuit of his characteristic opponent, the *retiarius*, or "net-man," an unhelmeted gladiator who carried a net and trident. For other gladiators, see **20, 36** and **58**. The first two words above stand alone. Translate: "To Amabilis the Secutor."

> **Amabili**: dat. sing. of Amabilis, Amabilis, m., *Amabilis*.
> **secutori**: dat. sing. of secutor, -oris, m., *secutor*.
> **nat(ione)**: abl. sing. of natio, nationis, m., *birth, nationality*.
> **Dacus**: Dacus, -a, -um, *Dacian, an inhabitant of Dacia*.
> **pugnavit**: "he fought."
> **fato**: fatum, -i, n., *fate*.
> **deceptus**: "having been foiled," "having been cheated," masc. nom., sing.
> **fato deceptus**: a phrase used to denote a natural death.

38. An Accomplished Woman (*CIL* 11.6249, 4-5)

**DOCTA LYRA GRATA ET GESTV FORMOSA PVELLA
HIC IACET AETERNA SABIS HVMATA DOMO**

**Docta lyrā, grata et gestu, formosa puella hīc iacet
aeternā Sabis humata domo.**

From an inscription found at Fanum Fortunae (Fano, Italy). The deceased, Sabis, is praised for both her physical beauty and her talents as a musician and performer. On women and the arts, see **66**.

> **docta**: doctus, -a, -um, *learned, accomplished*.
> **lyrā**: lyra, -ae, f., *the lyre; lyric poetry*.
> **gestu**: abl. sing. of gestus, -us, m., *posture; the gestures of a performer*.
> **formosa**: formosus, -a, -um, *beautiful*.
> **Sabis**: Sabis, Sabinis, f., *Sabis*.
> **humata**: "having been buried," fem. nom. sing.
> **domo**: domus, -us, f., *home*. Abl. of place where, but without a
>   preposition. The word domus often exhibits 2nd decl. endings as
>   here.

39. Good…and Good-looking (*CIL* 12.533, 3-8; Courtney 119)

VNO
MINVS QVAM BIS DENOS EGO VIXI PER ANNOS
INTEGER INNOCVVS SEMPER PIA MENTE
PROBATVS · QVI DOCILI LVSV IVVENVM
BENE DOCTVS HARENIS · PVLCHER ET ILLE FVI
VARIIS CIRCVMDATVS ARMIS

**Uno minus quam bis denos ego vixi per annos
integer, innocuus, semper piā mente probatus, qui
docili lusu iuvenum bene doctus harenis pulcher et
ille fui variis circumdatus armis.**

From a gravestone found at Aquae Sextiae (Aix-en-Provence, France). See also
133. From the rest of the inscription we know that it marked the grave of one
Sextus Julius Felicissimus, a member of the local group of *Iuvenes* ("Youths"),
an order of young men who did their military training together, paraded in
festivals, and exhibited their skills in shows. Ironically, this particular youth
not only hunted animals in the arena, but served as a veterinarian to them. In
addition to these talents, he was also well known, apparently, for his physical
beauty. The words above are spoken by the deceased.

> **uno**: masc. abl. sing. of unus, -a, -um, *one.*
> **minus quam**: "less than."
> **bis**: bis, adv., *twice, two times.*
> **denos**: deni, -ae, -a, *ten at a time, ten.*
> **vixi**: "I lived."
> **integer**: integer, -gra, -grum, *uncorrupted, upright.*
> **innocuus**: innocuus, -a, -um, *innocent, blameless.*
> **piā**: pius, -a, -um, *dutiful, patriotic, godly, kind.*
> **mente**: abl. sing. of mens, mentis, f., *mind, judgement, disposition.*
> **probatus**: "having been approved," "approved," masc. nom. sing.
> **qui**: "who," referring to the subject of **vixi**, "I," and subject of **fui**.
> **docili**: masc. abl. sing. of docilis, -e, *teachable, skilful.*
> **lusu**: abl. sing. of lusus, -us, m., *game, sport.*
> **iuvenum**: gen. plur. of iuvenis, iuvenis, c., *young man, young woman*;
>   *member of the* Iuvenes.
> **bene**: "well."
> **doctus**: doctus, -a, -um, *learned, accomplished.*
> **harenis**: harena, -ae, f., *sand; the arena in the amphitheatre* (because it
>   was covered with sand). Here, ablative of place where, but without a
>   preposition.
> **pulcher et ille fui**: "was also that 'Good-looker,'" (transl. Courtney).
> **circumdatus**: "having been girt," "equipped," masc. nom. sing.

40. A Brief Flowering (*CIL* 5.5320, 4-8)

VITA · BREVIS · LONGO · MELIOR · MORTA
LIBVS · AEVO · NAM · PARVO · SPATIO
FLORVIT · HAEC · ANIMA · BIS · DENOS
PERFVNCTA · ANNOS · SINE · CRIMINE
MORVM

**Vita brevis longo melior mortalibus aevo, nam
parvo spatio floruit haec anima bis denos perfuncta
annos sine crimine morum.**

From a gravestone found at Comum (Como, Italy), but now lost. A somewhat difficult thought expressed in condensed style. The composer asserts that a short life is better than a long one because it presents fewer opportunities to do dishonorable things that might sully one's good name. While somewhat strange to modern ears, this idea is grounded in the great value that the Romans placed on reputation. In the lines above, *haec anima* ("this soul") refers to the deceased.

brevis: fem. nom. sing. of brevis, -e, *brief, short.*
melior: "better," predicate with **vita** (understand **est**).
aevo: aevum, -i, n., *time, period of time, time of life, age.*
parvo: parvus, -a, -um, *small.*
spatio: spatium, -i, n., *interval, span of time.*
floruit: "flourished," "blossomed."
haec: fem. nom. sing. of hic, haec, hoc, *this.*
bis: bis, adv., *twice, two times.*
denos: deni, -ae, -a, *ten at a time, ten.*
perfuncta: "having completed," modifies **haec anima**.
crimine: abl. sing. of crimen, criminis, n., *charge, blame, crime.*
morum: gen. plur. of mos, moris, m., *habit, way;* (plur.) *character.*

41. Life and Afterlife (*CIL* 5.5278)

MORBORVM
VITIA ET VITAE
MALA MAXIMA
FVGI
NVNC CAREO
POENIS PACE
FRVOR PLACIDA

Morborum vitia et vitae mala maxima fugi.
Nunc careo poenis, pace fruor placidā.

Inscription from the side of a gravestone found at Comum (Como, Italy). An accompanying inscription identifies the deceased as Publius Ateilius Septicianus, a *grammaticus*, that is, a scholar and teacher of Latin language and literature. On the work of a *grammaticus*, see Juvenal, *Satire 7*, who cites such difficult conditions as long hours, impossibly high standards, and threats of legal action. The inscription notes that on his death, Ateilius "willed that his entire estate be transferred to the ownership of the republic." This must not have amounted to much: Juvenal remarks derisively that a *grammaticus* earned in a year what a charioteer earned in one race!

> **morborum**: morbus, -i, m., *sickness, disease.*
> **vitia**: vitium, -i, n., *fault; defect, weakness.*
> **maxima**: neut. acc. plur. of maximus, -a, -um, *greatest, very great.*
> **fugi**: "I have escaped."
> **careo**: careo, carēre (+ abl.), *to lack, to be without.*
> **poenis**: poena, -ae, f., *punishment, hardship.*
> **pace**: abl. sing. of pax, pacis, f., *peace.*
> **fruor**: fruor, frui (+ abl.), *to enjoy.*

42. A Decent Man (*CIL* 4.6626, 2; Wallace I.42)

LVCRETIVS HIC FRONTO DIGNVS HONORE BONO EST

Lucretius hic Fronto dignus honore bono est.

A dipinto from Pompeii. Election posters supporting Marcus Lucretius Fronto for the position of aedile have been found elsewhere in Pompeii, as well as an endorsement of him as a *vir fortis*, a "brave man" or perhaps "a man firm in his resolve." The line above follows a previous line which reads, "If decency is thought to confer any benefit in life...." For another election poster, see **153**.

hic: masc. nom. sing. of hic, haec, hoc, *this.*
Lucretius Fronto: *Lucretius Fronto.*
dignus: dignus, -a, -um, *worthy of* (+ abl.).
honore: abl. sing. of honor, -oris, m., *honor, esteem; public office, career.*

43. To Claudia (*CIL* 1².1211; 6.15346; Courtney 17)

HOSPES · QVOD · DEICO · PAVL{L}VM · EST · ASTA · AC · PELLEGE
HEIC · EST · SEPVLCRVM · HAV · PVLCRVM · PVLCRAI · FEMINAE
NOMEN · PARENTES · NOMINARVNT · CLAVDIAM
SVOM · MAREITVM · CORDE · DEILEXIT · SOVO
GNATOS · DVOS · CREAVIT · HORVNC · ALTERVM
IN · TERRA · LINQVIT · ALIVM · SVB · TERRA · LOCAT
SERMONE · LEPIDO · TVM · AVTEM · INCESSV · COMMODO
DOMVM · SERVAVIT · LANAM · FECIT · DIXI · ABEI

**Hospes, quod d*i*co paulum est, asta ac perlege. H*ī*c
est sepulcrum hau<d> pulc<h>rum pulc<h>ra*e*
feminae. Nomen parentes nomina(ve)runt
Claudiam. Su*u*m mar*i*tum corde d*i*lexit s*u*o. Natos
duos creavit; horu*m* alterum in terrā linquit, alium
sub terrā locat. Sermone lepido, tum autem incessu
commodo. Domum servavit, lanam fecit. dixi. Ab*i*.**

An inscription discovered in Rome, but now lost. One of the oldest inscriptions in this book (2nd century BC), it features a number of archaic spellings (compare **139**, from the same period). Also noteworthy are several wordplays which juxtapose words that are (or were thought to be) etymologically related—e.g., *sepulcrum/pulchrum*; *nomen/nominarunt*. In addition, this is an example of a "talking inscription"—the stone itself is the subject of the verbs *dico* and *dixi* (see also **122**). Judging from the evidence of this well-known epitaph, what are the characteristics that Romans of the period valued in women? The words above are addressed to anyone who happens to be passing by the monument.

hospes: voc. sing. of hospes, hospitis, m., *guest, host, stranger, passerby.*
quod: "what," dir. obj. of **dico** and subject of **est**.
paulum: paulus, -a, -um, *little, small, short.*
asta ac perlege: "stop and read (it) carefully."
hau<d>: haud, adv., *by no means.*
sepulcrum: sepulcrum, -i, n., *grave, tomb.*
nomen: acc. sing. of nomen, -inis, n., *name.*
parentes: nom. plur. of parens, parentis, c., *parent.*
nomina(ve)runt: "named," or, with **nomen** as dir. obj., "gave (her) the name."

suum: suus, -a, -um, *his (own), her (own), its (own), their (own)*.
maritum: maritus, -i, m., *husband*.
corde: abl. sing. of cor, cordis, n., *heart*.
dilexit: "she loved."
suo: see **suum** above.
natos: natus, -i, m., *son*.
creavit: "she bore."
horum: masc. gen. plur. of hic, haec, hoc, *this*: "of these."
alterum: alter, altera, alterum, *one* (of two); *the other* (of two).
linquit: linquo, linquere, *to leave* (transitive), *to leave behind*.
alium: alius, -a, -um, *other, another; the one; the other*.
locat: loco, locare: *to place*.
sermone: abl. sing. of sermo, sermonis, m., *speech, conversation*.
lepido: lepidus, -a, -um, *pleasant*.
tum autem: "and also."
incessu: abl. sing. of incessus, -us, m., *bearing, gait*.
commodo: commodus, -a, -um, *agreeable, pleasing*.
servavit: "she maintained."
lanam: lana, -ae, f., *wool*.
fecit: "she made."
dixi: "I have spoken."
abi: "depart."

PART 2

Verbs: The Forms
of the Indicative and Imperative

IV. Present System, Indicative

For verbs forms in the present active system, see Part 1.

V. Present System, Imperative

44. Beware of the Dog (*CIL* 10.877)

CAVE CANEM

—❦—

Cave canem!

—❦—

Mosaic at the entrance of the House of the Tragic Poet in Pompeii.

cave: caveo, -ēre, *to beware of, watch out for.*
canem: acc. sing. of canis, canis, c., *dog.*

29

45. Good Hygiene

BENE LAVA

Bene lava!

An encouragement often found spelled out in mosaic tiles at the entrance to baths.

> **bene**: "well."
> **lava**: lavo, -are, -avi, -atum, *to wash, bathe.*

46. Wealth Always Welcome (*CIL* 10.874)

SALVE · LVCRV

Salve, lucru<m>!

Mosaic floor pavement from Pompeii.

> **salve**: salveo, -ēre, *to be well*; (imperat.) *hello!*
> **lucru<m>**: lucrum, -i, n., *profit.*

47. Too Much Free Time? (*CIL* IV.2069)

MORAM SI QVAERES, SPARGE MILIV ET COL LIGE

Moram si quaeres, sparge miliu<m> et collige.

Graffito from Pompeii.

> **moram**: mora, -ae, f., *delay; a way to waste time.*
> **si**: *if.*
> **quaeres**: quaero, -ere, *to seek, ask, inquire.*
> **sparge**: spargo, -ere, *to scatter.*
> **miliu<m>**: milium, -i, n., *millet* (a kind of grain).
> **collige**: colligo, -ere, *to gather, pick up.*

48. Lullaby (from a scholiast's note on Persius *Satires* III.16)

Lalla, lalla, lalla,
aut dormi aut lacte.

Neither an inscription or a graffito, this text comes from a later copyist's note on a word used by the 1st c. AD poet Persius. Providing a fascinating glimpse inside the Roman household, the copyist explains that these words were often sung to infants to help them fall asleep.

> **aut...aut:** either...or.
> **dormi:** dormio, -ire, *to sleep.*
> **lacte:** lacteo, -ēre, *to suckle, nurse.*

49. Unwelcome Visitor (*CIL* 4.5112)

DISCITE DVM VIVO MORS
INIMICA VENIS

Discite: Dum vivo, Mors inimica, venis.

Graffito from Pompeii.

> **discite:** disco, -ere, *to learn, get to know, come to understand.*
> **dum:** "while."
> **vivo:** vivo, -ere, *to live, be alive.*
> **Mors:** mors, mortis, f., *death.*
> **inimica:** inimicus, -a, -um, *unfriendly, hateful.*
> **venis:** venio, -ire, *to come, arrive.*

VI. Perfect System, Indicative Active

50. No Worries (*CIL* 5.2893, 5)

N · F · F·N · S · N · C

N(on) f(ui), f(ui), n(on) s(um), n(on) c(uro).

From an epitaph found in Patavium (Padua, Italy). This highly abbreviated line can be confidently interpreted on the basis of numerous examples of the same or similar sentiment which have been found on other gravestones. Graffito from Pompeii.

> **c(uro):** curo, -are, -avi, -atum, *to care, care for/about.*

51. Playful Agathe (*CIL* 6.19007, 5)

DVM VIXI LVSI

Dum vixi, lusi.

From an epitaph found in Rome commemorating Geminia Agathe, a girl who lived 5 years and 7 months.

> **vixi:** vivo, -ere, vixi, victum, *to live, be alive.*
> **lusi:** ludo, -ere, lusi, lusum, *to play.*

52. Missing Urbana (*CIL* 4.2146; Wallace II.124)

**VIBIVS RESTITVTVS HIC
SOLVS · DORMIVIT ET VRBANAM
SVAM DESIDERABAT**

**Vibius Restitutus hīc solus dormivit et Urbanam
suam desiderabat.**

A graffito from the wall of an inn at Pompeii. Considering the reputation of inns in the Roman world, the fidelity of this particular guest is commendable. It is uncertain whether this is the same Restitutus who is accused of infidelity in **5**. For other inscriptions relating to inns, see **10**, **54** and **61**.

> **Vibius Restitutus:** *Vibius Restitutus.*
> **solus:** solus, -a, -um, *alone.*
> **Urbanam:** Urbana, -ae, f., *Urbana.*
> **suam:** suus, -a, -um, *his (own), her (own), its (own), their (own).*
> **desiderabat:** desidero, -are, -avi, -atum, *to long for, miss.*

53. A Good Student (*CIL* 6.12013, 7-10)

**STVDIA
AMAVI · OBSEQVENS · MAGISTRIS · FVI
OBSERVAVI · PARENTORVM · PRAECEPTA · ME
[OS A]MICOS COLVI**

**Studia amavi, obsequens magistris fui, observavi
parentorum praecepta, meos amicos colui.**

Fragmentary gravestone, found at Rome, now lost. The earlier part of the inscription marks this as the grave of Antonius Severus Aquila, who lived "12 years, 16 months." Obedience to parents and teachers is a virtue commonly cited in the epitaphs of children. But although teachers were not averse to using the rod (see, e.g., Martial, *Epigrams* X.62; Horace, *Epistles*, I.70), obedience cannot have been universal (see, e.g., **27**!).

> **obsequens**: obsequens, -ntis, *yielding, compliant, obedient.*
> **observavi**: observo, -are, -avi, -atum, *to pay attention to, heed.*
> **parentorum**: parens, usually a third declension noun, is here given a second declension ending.
> **praecepta**: praeceptum, -i, n., *lesson, teaching, command.*
> **colui**: colo, colere, colui, cultum, *inhabit, cultivate; honor, cherish, worship.*

54. Not my Fault (*CIL* 4.4957; Courtney 73; Wallace II.200)

MIXIMVS IN LECTO FATEOR PECCAVIMVS
HOSPES SI DICES QVARE NVLLA METELLA FVIT

Miximus in lecto; fateor, peccavimus,
hospes. Si dices "quare?," nulla metella fuit.

A graffito from Pompeii, explaining why a guest has had an accident in bed. For other inscriptions relating to inns, see **10**, **52**, and **61**.

> **miximus**: mingo, mingere, minxi (or mixi), mictum, *to urinate.* Plural, but to be translated as singular here.
> **lecto**: lectus, -i, m., *couch, bed.*
> **fateor**: "I admit."
> **peccavimus**: pecco, peccare, peccavi, peccatum, *to make a mistake, to do wrong.* Translate as singular.
> **hospes**: hospes, hospitis, m., *guest, host, stranger, passerby* (here, a particular sort of host, an *innkeeper*).
> **quare**: quare, adv., *why*
> **metella**: metella, -ae, f., *chamber-pot.*

55. Reward for My Return (*CIL* 15.7194)

**FVGI TENE ME
CVM REVOCV
VERIS ME · DM ·
ZONINO ACCIPIS
SOLIDVM ·**

**Fugi. Tene me. Cum revoc*a*veris me d(omino) m(eo)
Zonino, accipis solidum.**

A slave collar from Rome, now in the National Museum of Rome at the Baths of Diocletian. Not uncommon in the late Roman period, these collars identified the wearer as a slave and often gave information about where the slave should be returned if caught as a fugitive. The narrow elongated letter forms are characteristic of inscriptions dating from the 4th to 6th centuries AD. For another slave collar, see **135**.

cum: "when."
revoc*a*veris: fut. perf. indic. of revoco, -are, -avi, -atum, *bring back*.
d(omino): Classical Latin would use the accusative with a preposition
    (see, e.g., **135**).

Zonino: Zoninus, -i, m., *Zoninus*, a proper name.
accipis: "you will receive." In Latin, the present tense is sometimes used for the future. Compare English: "What are you doing tonight?"
solidum: solidus, -i, m., *a solidus* (i.e., *aureus solidus*, a gold coin).

56. Tragic Reversal (*CIL* 8.8567, 1)

GAVDIA QVE DEDERAT RAPVIT FORTVNA REPENTE

Gaudia, qu<a>e dederat, rapuit Fortuna repente.

From a gravestone found at Sitifis in North Africa (Tunisia). What conception of human life is implied by this sentiment?

gaudia: gaudium, -i, n., *joy, pleasure.*
qu<a>e: "which," referring to **gaudia**, and dir. obj. of **dederat**.
rapuit: rapio, rapere, rapui, raptum, *to seize, snatch away.*
repente: repente, adv., *suddenly.*

57. Zmyrna, Age 7 (*CIL* 6.23629, 7)

ANIMA MEA RAPVERVNT FATA INIQVA

Anima<m> mea<m> rapuerunt fata iniqua.

From an epitaph inscribed on a marble tablet found in Rome. For "unjust fates," see also **8**. The deceased, Zmyrna, is to be understood as speaking the line above.

iniqua: iniquus, -a, -um, *adverse, unfair.*

58. To a Long-lived Gladiator (*CIL* 6.10195)

DI{I}S MANIBVS
M · ANTONIO · NIGRO
VETERANO · THRAECI
QVI · VIX · ANN · XXXVIII ·
PVGNAVIT XVIII
FLAVIA · DIOGENIS ·
CONIVGI · SVO · BENE
MERENTI ·
DE · SVO · FECIT

Dis Manibus. M(arco) Antonio Nigro, veterano
Thraeci, qui vix(it) ann(os) XXXVIII, pugnavit
XVIII. Flavia Diogenis coniugi suo bene merenti de
suo fecit.

An epitaph found in Rome. The long career of this gladiator does not necessarily imply that he was undefeated. The economics of the games did not permit every match to be to the death. The epitaph of another gladiator, for instance, records a record of 21 wins, 4 losses, and 9 ties (*CIL* 10.7297). For other gladiators, see **20**, **36** and **37**.

Dis Manibus: "To the Departed Spirits," a common introductory invocation in Roman epitaphs.

M(arco) Antonio Nigro: *Marcus Antonius Niger*. Here in the dative case with no governing verb. Translate "To Marcus Antonius Niger..."

veterano: veteranus, -a, -um, *veteran*.

Thraeci: Thraex (also spelled Thrax), Thraecis, *Thracian*. For this gladiatorial type, see **20**.

qui: "who," subject of **vix(it)** and **pugnavit**.

Flavia Diogenis: *Flavia Diogenis*.

coniugi: coniunx, coniugis, c., *spouse*.

suo: suus, -a, -um, *his (own), her (own), its (own), their (own)*.

bene merenti: "well deserving," modifies **coniugi**.

de suo: "from her own (resources)."

59. Fuscus the Charioteer (*CIL* 2.4315, 2-13; Courtney 112)

FACTIONIS · VENETAE · FVSCO · SACRA
VIMVS · ARAM · DE · NOSTRO · CERTI · STV
DIOSI ET BENE AMANTES · VT SCI
RENT CVNCTI MONIMENTVM
ET PIGNVS AMORIS · INTEG[RA]
FAMA · TIBI · LAVDEM · CVR
SVS · MERVISTI · CERTASTI
MVLTIS · NVLLVM PAVPER TI[MV]
ISTI · I[NVIDIAM PASSVS SEM]
[PER FORTIS TACVISTI] · PVL
CHRE VIXISTI FATO MORTA
LIS OBISTI

**Factionis Venetae Fusco sacravimus aram de nostro,
certi studiosi et bene amantes, ut scirent cuncti
mon*u*mentum et pignus amoris. Integra fama tibi,
laudem cursus meruisti, certa(vi)sti multis, nullum
pauper timuisti, invidiam passus semper fortis
tacuisti, pulchre vixisti, fato mortalis obi*i*sti.**

From an epitaph found at Tarraco (Tarragona, Spain), a city large enough to have had a *circus*, an oblong track where chariot races were conducted. The first two words of the inscription identify Fuscus as a member of the Blue Team, one of the four teams, or factions (the others being Green, Red, and White), into which charioteers and their crews were organized.

> **factionis**: factio, factionis, f., *team, faction.*
> **Venetae**: venetus, -a, -um, *blue.*
> **Fusco**: Fuscus, -i, m., *Fuscus.*
> **sacravimus**: sacro, -are, -avi, -atum, *to dedicate.*
> **aram**: ara, -ae, f., *altar, altar-tomb.*
> **de nostro**: "from our own (resources)."
> **certi**: certus, -a, -um, *certain, steadfast, loyal.*
> **studiosi**: studiosus, -a, -um, *eager, devoted*, here as a substantive, "fans."
> **bene amantes**: "enthusiastic," "devoted," modifies **studiosi**.
> **ut scirent cuncti**: "so that all might know."
> **mon*u*mentum**: monumentum, -i, n., *monument, memorial, record.*
> **pignus**: pignus, -oris, n., *pledge, token, proof.*
> **amoris**: amor, amoris, m., *love, passion, devotion.*
> **integra**: integer, -gra, -grum, *uncorrupted, upright.* Predicate of an understood **est**.

fama: Subject of an understood **est.**

tibi: dat. sing. of tu, *you* (understand **est**).

laudem: laus, laudis, f., *praise, fame, glory.*

cursus: cursus, -us, m., *course; speed* (objective or causal gen. with **laudem**).

meruisti: mereo, -ēre, -ui, -itum, *to deserve, earn, obtain, win.*

certa(vi)sti: certo, -are, -avi, -atum, *to contend with, compete against.*

pauper: pauper, -eris, m., *a poor man* (here, concessive, "though a poor man").

invidiam passus: "though you suffered envy."

obiisti: obeo, -ire, -ii, itum, *to go to meet; to go to meet death, to die* (with **fato**, "to die a natural death").

VII. Present System, Indicative Passive

60. To Love and Be Loved (*CIL* IV.4637; Wallace II.131)

CORNELIA · HELE[NA]
AMATVR AB · RVFO

Cornelia Helena amatur ab Rufo.

A graffito from Pompeii.

Cornelia Helena: *Cornelia Helena.*

Rufo: Rufus, -i, m., *Rufus.*

61. Eat Here (*CIL* 4.807; Wallace I.78)

HOSPITIVM · HIC · LOCATVR
TRICLINIVM · CVM · TRIBVS · LECTIS

Hospitium hīc locatur. Triclinium cum tribus lectis.

A dipinto from Pompeii. This advertisement identified the inn in question as a high class establishment. While some inns offered only rooms for spending the night and others provided facilities for standing or seated meals, the better ones could boast of couches upon which diners could recline. Houses at Pompeii and elsewhere attest to the Romans' predilection for dining rooms with couches arranged on three sides of a low table. For other inscriptions relating to inns, see **10, 52,** and **54.**

hospitium: hospitium, -i, n., *hospitality; an inn, lodging.*

locatur: loco, -are, *to put, place, locate.*
triclinium: triclinium, -i, n., *dining room.*
tribus: tres, tria, *three.*
lectis: lectus, -i, m., *couch, bed.*

62. To See My Brother (*CIL* 3.14850, 10)

IAM TRAHOR IN TENEBRAS DVCORQ·AMPLECTERE FRATR

Iam trahor in tenebras ducorq(ue) amplectere fratr(em).

From an inscription found near Salonae (Split, Croatia). The inscription commemorates a pair of deceased brothers curiously named Quintus Septimius Antonius and Quintus Septimius Antoninus, aged 18 and 22 years respectively. In the line above, one of these brothers describes where death is taking him. What view of the afterlife is implied by this sentiment?

trahor: traho, trahere, *to drag.*
tenebras: tenebrae, -arum, f., *darkness.*
amplectere: "to embrace," irregular pres. infin. of amplector. The infinitive is used to express purpose here—a usage rare in Classical authors.

63. The Rape of Deianira (*CIL* 13.10013a)

CENTAVRO VEHITVR RAPTA DEIA[N]IRA MARITO

Centauro vehitur rapta Deianira marito.

Found written in a circular pattern on an earthenware plate from Colonia Agrippina (Cologne, Germany). The text serves as a caption for the myth pictured on the plate: Nessus, having seized Hercules's wife Deianira, is shown fleeing from Hercules, who is aiming his arrow at the rapacious Centaur.

Centauro: Centaurus, -i, m., *a Centaur,* a monster half-man and half-horse. Ablative of agent without the preposition *a/ab,* or ablative of means?
vehitur: veho, vehere, *to carry.*
rapta: "having been seized," fem. nom. sing.
Deianira: Deianira, -ae, f., *Deianira,* the wife of Hercules.
marito: dative or ablative of separation with **rapta**.

64. Reduced to This (*CIL* 6.37965, 5; Gordon 65)

SERIOLA · PARVA · TAM MAGNA · TENERIS

Seriolā parvā tam magna teneris.

From the long epitaph, inscribed on a large marble tablet found in Rome, of Allia Potestas, a freedwoman from Perugia. See also **82**. Elsewhere in the inscription, her many virtues are described in extravagant detail (including her diligence, courage, purity, tenacity, and cleanliness), along with her beauty (radiant complexion, beautiful eyes, golden hair, and legs like the mythological Atalanta's). In the line above, her greatness (or, perhaps, great size) in life is contrasted with the small jar in which her ashes now repose.

seriolā: seriola, -ae, f., *jar*.

65. To Aeonius (*CIL* 5.6693, 4-5)

SIC · FORTVNA · TIBI · DEDERAT · TRANSCVRRERE · VITAM
OMNES · MORTALES · EADEM · NAM · SORTE · TENEMVR

Sic Fortuna tibi dederat transcurrere vitam,
omnes mortales eādem nam sorte tenemur.

From a gravestone found at Vercellae (Vercelli, Italy). The words are addressed to the deceased. What view of life is implied by this sentiment? What view of death?

eādem: fem. abl. sing. of idem, eadem, idem, *the same*.
nam: adv., *for*. Translate before **omnes mortales**.
sorte: sors, sortis, f., *lot, fate*.

66. Eucharis (*CIL* 1².1214, 20-21; 6.10096; Courtney 20)

BIS · HIC · SEPTENI · MECVM · NATALES DIES
TENEBRIS · TENENTVR · DITIS · AETERNA DOM[V]

Bis hīc septeni mecum natales dies tenebris tenentur
Ditis aeternā domu.

From an epitaph found inscribed on a marble tablet in Rome. Elsewhere in the inscription it is said that the deceased, Eucharis, was a girl "educated, as it were, at the hands of the Muses," who performed before the people on "the Greek stage." The precise meaning of this is not clear, but it most likely identifies her as a singer and dancer of some kind. While Roman men appreciated the cultivation of the arts by their wives and daughters, performance on the stage was considered beneath a free-born woman. Under Augustus, for instance, marriage was forbidden between men of senatorial rank and women who had performed on stage. Eucharis is to be understood as speaking the lines cited above.

> **bis**: bis, adv., *twice, two times.*
> **septeni**: septeni, -ae, -a, *seven at a time, seven.*
> **natales**: natalis, -e, *having to do with birth* (*natalis dies* = "birthday").
> **tenebris**: "in the darkness."
> **Ditis**: Dis, Ditis, m., *Dis,* another name for Pluto, god of the underworld.
> **domu**: domus, -us, f., *home.* Abl. of place where, but without a
> preposition.

67. Apollonia (*CIL* 9.2272, 2-3)

APOLLONIA · QVAE · VOCITABAR
LAPIDE · HOC · INCLVSA · QVIESCO

Apollonia quae vocitabar, lapide hōc inclusa quiesco.

From an epitaph found at Telesia (Telese Terme, Italy).

> **Apollonia**: Apollonia, -ae, f., *Apollonia.* Predicate with **vocitabar**.
> **quae**: "who," subject of **vocitabar**.
> **vocito**: vocito, -are, *to call, name.*
> **lapide**: abl. sing. of lapis, lapidis, m., *stone.*
> **inclusa**: "enclosed," fem. nom. sing.

VIII.   Perfect System, Indicative Passive

68. Dedication to Julius Caesar (*CIL* 1².797; 6.872; Gordon 21)

DIVO · IVLIO · IVSSV
POPVLI · ROMANI
STATVTVM · EST · LEGE
RVFRENA

Divo Iulio iussu populi Romani statutum est lege
Rufrena.

From what is probably a statue base, found at Ocriculum (Otricoli, Italy), and now in the Vatican Museum. The *Lex Rufrena* ("Law proposed by Rufrenus") provided for the erection of statues of Julius Caesar throughout Italy. This particular statue was erected around the time of Caesar's assassination in 44 BC.

divo: divus, -a, -um, *divine; deified.*
iussu: "by order."
statutum est: statuo, statuere, statui, statutum, *to put up, erect* (understand "this (monument)" as subject).
lege: lex, legis, f., *law.*
Rufrena: adj. from the proper name *Rufrenus*. Translate **lege Rufrena** as "in accordance with the Law of Rufrenus."

69. Helvia Prima (*CIL* 1².1732, 7; 9.1837)

NVNC DATA SVM DITI LONGVM MANSVRA PER AEVM

Nunc data sum Diti, longum mansura per ae<v>um.

From an epitaph found at Beneventum (Benevento, Italy). See also **146**. The deceased, Helvia Prima, is to be understood as speaking the line. What conception of the afterlife is implied by this sentiment?

> **Diti**: Dis, Ditis, m., *Dis*, another name for Pluto, god of the underworld.
> **mansura**: fem. nom. sing. fut. act. participle of maneo, manēre, mansi, mansum, *to remain, stay, endure*. Translate: "to endure."
> **ae<v>um**: aevum, -i, n., *time, period of time, time of life, age*.

70. Zoticus (*CIL* 9.2042q)

ZOTICVS · HIC · NOMEN · NVDVM
VANVMQ · RELIQVIT
IN · CINERES · CORPVS · ET · IN · AETHERA
VITA · SOLVTA · EST

Zoticus hīc nomen nudum vanumq(ue) reliquit.
In cineres corpus et in aethera vita soluta est.

A gravestone found at Beneventum (Benevento, Italy), now lost. What conception of the afterlife is implied by this sentiment?

> **Zoticus**: Zoticus, -i, m., *Zoticus*.
> **vanum**: vanus, -a, -um, *empty*.
> **cineres**: cinis, -eris, m., *ashes*.
> **aethera**: acc. sing. of aether, aetheris, m., *upper air, sky; heaven*. This word, like others of Greek origin, retains an acc. sing. ending akin to the Greek form.
> **soluta est**: solvo, -ere, solvi, solutum, *loosen, release, free; scatter*. With both **corpus** and **vita** as subjects, although it agrees grammatically only with the latter.

71. Death of a Grain Merchant (*CIL* 1².2965; Gordon 20; Keppie, p. 98)

SEX · AEMILIVS · SEX · L
BARO
FRVMENTAR
INIGNEM · INLATVS · EST
PRID · NONQVINCT
CN · POMPEIO · COS · TERT

**Sex(tus) Aemilius Sex(ti) l(ibertus) Baro,
frumentar(ius), in ignem inlatus est prid(ie) Non(as)
Quinct(iles), Gn(aeo) Pompeio co(n)s(ule) tert(ium).**

A marble slab found in Rome. The reference to the third consulship of Gnaeus
Pompeius (Pompey the Great) dates the inscription to 52 BC. The Romans
practiced both cremation (burning the dead) and inhumation (burying the
dead), with one practice or the other being dominant during various periods. In
this inscription the process of cremation is described in unusually vivid terms.
For more on cremation, see **137**. This freedman's epitaph also provides a piece of
information that the Romans rarely included: the actual date of death.

> **Sex(tus) Aemilius…Baro**: *Sextus Aemilius Baro*.
> **libertus**: libertus, -i, m., *freedman*.
> **frumentarius**: frumentarius, -i, m., *grain merchant*.
> **inlatus est**: infero, inferre, intuli, inlatum, *to bring in, place on*.
> **prid(ie) Non(as) Quinct(iles)**: the day before the *Nones* of *Quinctilis*,
> or July 6. (Note that the month of *Quinctilis* (or, more usually,
> *Quintilis*) was not renamed *Iulius* ("July") in honor of Julius Caesar
> until 44 BC).
> **Gn(aeo) Pompeio co(n)s(ule) tert(ium)**: "in the third consulship of
> Gnaeus Pompeius."

72. Mother and Son (*CIL* 6.12202, 5-6)

IN · HAC · CVPA
MATER · ET · FILIVS · POSITI · SVNT

In hac cupā mater et filius positi sunt.

From an epitaph found in Rome, commissioned by Decius Apuleius Ionicus for
his sister and her son.

> **cupā**: cupa, -ae, f., *niche*, a hollow in a wall for placing the ashes of the
> dead, or possibly used here as a synonym for *sepulcrum* (tomb).

PART 3

Miscellaneous Forms and Constructions

IX. Relative Clause

73. Nine Years, More or Less (*CIL* 6.19217, 2-4)

**HELPIDIAE · BENE · MERENTI ·
QVAE · VIXIT · PLVS · MINVS ·
ANNIS ·   IX·**

Helpidiae, bene merenti, quae vixit plus minus annis IX.

From an epitaph found in Rome. While some epitaphs mark the duration of the deceased's life to the hour (see, e.g., **90**), others, like this one, are less precise.

    Helpidiae: Helpidia, -ae, f., *Helpidia*.
    bene merenti: "well deserving," dat. sing. fem.
    annis: Occasionally in later Latin the ablative, not the accusative, is used
       to express duration of time. See also **108**.

74. Drink Up (*CIL* 3.293, 2-4)

DVM · VIXI
[BI]BI · LIBENTER · BIBI[TE] · VOS
QVI · VIVITIS

Dum vixi, bibi libenter. Bibite vos qui vivitis.

From an epitaph found at Antioch in Pisidia (Turkey), marking the grave of Titus Cissonius, a veteran legionary in the Roman army. What view of life and death is implied by this sentiment? Compare **75**, **76**, and **123**. The deceased is to be understood as speaking the line.

> **dum**: "while." Although dum + pres. indic. is typically used to denote continued action in past time, dum + a past tense of the indicative may be used to draw a strong contrast, as here. See also **147**.
> **libenter**: libenter, adv., *willingly, gladly, with pleasure.*
> **bibite**: bibo, bibere, bibi, bibitum, *drink.*

75. The Lucky Living (*CIL* 6.28239, 8)

VIVITE · FELICES · SVPERI · QVORVM · FORTVNA · BEATAST

Vivite felices, superi, quorum fortuna beata (e)st.

From an epitaph found in Rome. What view of life and death is implied by this sentiment? Compare **74**, **76**, and **123**. The deceased is to be understood as speaking the line.

> **felices**: felix, felicis, *happy, joyful, blessed; lucky, prosperous.*
> **superi**: superi, -orum, m., *gods above; humans on earth.*
> **beata**: beatus, -a, -um, *blessed, happy.*

76. Be Happy (*CIL* 13.6858, 9-10)

VIVITE FELIC[ES Q]VIBVS · EST ·
DATA · VITA · FRVEND[A]

Vivite felices, quibus est data vita fruenda.

From an inscription found near Moguntiacum (Mainz, Germany). What view of life and death is implied by this sentiment? Compare **74**, **75**, and **123**. The deceased is to be understood as speaking the line.

> **felices**: felix, felicis, *happy, joyful, blessed; lucky, prosperous.*
> **est data**: **data est**
> **fruenda**: "to be enjoyed."

77. Riddle (*CIL* 11.6243, 6-8)

VIATOR · VIATOR · QVOD · TV
ES · EGO · FVI · QVOD · NVNC · SVM
ET · TV· ERIS

Viator, viator, quod tu es, ego fui; quod nunc sum, et tu eris.

From an epitaph found at Fanum Fortunae (Fano, Italy).

> **viator**: viator, -oris, m., *traveler.*

78. Can't Take it With You? (*CIL* 6.18131, 1-8))

DM
T · FLAVIVS ·
MARTIALIS · HIC ·
SITVS · EST · QVOD · EDI
BIBI · MECVM · HABEO
QVOD · RELIQVI
PERDIDI
V · A · LXXX

D(is) M(anibus). T(itus) Flavius Martialis hic situs est. "Quod edi, bibi, mecum habeo; quod reliqui, perdidi." V(ixit) a(nnos) LXXX.

From an epitaph inscribed on a marble tablet found in Rome.

> **T(itus) Flavius Martialis**: *Titus Flavius Martialis.*
> **edi**: edo, edere, edi, esum, *to eat.*
> **bibi**: bibo, -ere, bibi, bibitum, *to drink.*
> **perdo**: perdo, -ere, -didi, -ditum, *to waste, lose; destroy.*

79. To Jupiter (*CIL* 8.17586)

[HA]NC · [T]IBI
QVAM VO
VI POSVI
BONE · IVP
P[I]TER ARAM
PRAEF COH
NOMINE
GALLONI
VS

**Hanc tibi quam vovi, posui, bone Iuppiter, aram
praef(ectus) coh(ortis) nomine Gallonius.**

Dedicatory inscription for an altar, found at Thelepte (Tunisia).

quam: a "proleptic" relative, because it precedes rather than follows its
antecedent **aram**.
vovi: voveo, vovēre, vovi, votus, *to dedicate, consecrate, vow.*
aram: ara, arae, f., *altar.*
praef(ectus): praefectus, -i, m., *commander, prefect.*
coh(ortis): cohors, cohortis, f., *cohort, tenth part of a legion.*
Gallonius: Gallonius, -i, m., *Gallonius.*

80. Denied (*CIL* 5.6128 7-8)

HIS · REQVIESCO · LOCIS · VITAM · CVI · FATA
NEGARVNT

His requiesco locis, vitam cui fata nega(ve)runt.

From an epitaph found at Mediolanum (Milan, Italy).

requiesco: requiesco, requiescere, requievi, requietus, *to rest.*
locis: locus, i, m., *place.* Plural, but translate as singular.
cui: note that **vitam** is placed outside of the relative clause to which it
belongs.
nega(ve)runt: nego, negare, negavi, negatum, *to deny, refuse.*

81. Poor Procope (*CIL* 6.25075)

PROCOPE · MANVS
LEBO CONTRA
DEVM QVI
ME INNOCEN
TEM SVSTVLIT
QVAE VXIT
ANN XX
POS PROCLVS

Procope manus *levo* contra Deum qui me innocentem
sustulit, quae v<i>xit ann(os) XX. Pos(uit) Proclus.

Epitaph inscribed on marble tablet found in Rome, now in the Vatican Museum.
There are two relative pronouns in the inscription. What is the antecedent of
each?

Procope: *Procope*, nominative singular.
levo: levo, -are, -avi, -atum, *to raise, lift up.*
sustulit: tollo, tollere, sustuli, sublatum, *to lift up, raise up, take away.*
Proclus: Proclus, -i, m., *Proclus.*

82. A Woman from Perugia (*CIL* 6.37965, 3-4; Gordon 65)

HIC · PERVSINA · SITA · EST · QVA · NON · PRETIOSIOR · VLLA
FEMINA

Hīc Perusina sita est, quā non pretiosior ulla femina.

From the epitaph of the freedwoman Allia Potestas, found in Rome. For more
on this inscription, see **64**.

Perusina: Perusinus, -a, -um, f., *Perusian, from Perusia* (Perugia, Italy).
sita: situs, -a, -um, *placed, situated, located.*
quā: "than whom."
pretiosior: "more precious."

83. Crushed to Death (*CIL* 6.29436, 1-3; Courtney 196)

VMMIDIAE · MANES · TVMVLVS · TEGIT ·
ISTE · SIMVLQVE · PRIMIGENI · VERNAE
QVOS · TVLIT · VNA · DIES

Ummidiae manes tumulus tegit iste, simulque
Primigeni vernae, quos tulit una dies.

From an epitaph found at Rome, marking the grave of Ummidia and a
house-born slave (*verna*) named Primigenius. The inscription also records
their manner of death—something not frequently found in Roman epitaphs.
Ummidia and Primigenius were crushed to death by a crowd on the Capitoline
Hill (*Capitolinae compressi examine turbae*).

Ummidiae: Ummidia, -ae, f., *Ummidia.*
manes: manes, -ium, m. *shades of the departed, spirits of the dead.*
tumulus: tumulus, -i, m., *burial mound.*
tegit: tego, tegere, texi, tectum, *to cover, bury.*
iste: iste, ista, istud, *that.*
simul: adv., *at the same time.*
Primigeni: Primigenius, -i, m., *Primigenius.*
vernae: verna, -ae, c., *house-born slave.*
tulit: fero, ferre, tuli, latus, *to carry, carry off, bear.*

84. Master Craftsman (*CIL* 12.722, 2-10; Courtney 132)

A[RS · CVI · SVM]MA · [FVIT]
FABRIC[AE · STVDIVM · DOCTRIN]
PVDOR · [QVE] QVEM · M[AGNI]
ARTIFI[CES] · SEMPER · DIX{S}ERE
MAGIST[RVM · DOCTIO]R · HOC · [NE]
MO · FVIT · [PO]T[VIT] · QVEM · VINC
ERE · NEMO · ORGANA · QVI · NOSSE
T · FACERE · AQVARVM · AVT · DVCE
RE CVRSVM

Ars cui summa fuit fabricae, studium, doctrin(a)
pudorque, quem magni artifices semper dixer*unt*
magistrum. Doctior hōc nemo fuit, potuit quem
vincere nemo, organa qui no(vi)sset facere aquarum
aut ducere cursum.

From an inscription on a sarcophagus found at Arelate (Arles, France). The rest of the inscription identifies the deceased as Quintus Candidius Benignus, a carpenter. On either side of the inscription are represented tools of the carpenter's trade: a plumb-line and an adze. Begin translation with "To Quintus Candidius Benignus…").

> **ars**: ars, artis, f., *art, craft; skill, expertise.*
> **cui**: dat. of possession. Note that **ars** is placed outside of the relative clause to which it belongs.
> **summa**: summus, -a, -um, *the highest.*
> **fabricae**: fabrica, -ae, f., *workmanship, craftsmanship.*
> **doctrin(a)**: doctrina, -ae, f., *learning, training.*
> **pudor**: pudor, pudoris, m., *modesty, decency, honor.*
> **artifices**: artifex, -ficis, m., *craftsman.*
> **doctior**: "more learned," "more skilled," masc., nom., sing.
> **hōc**: "than this man."
> **quem**: logically precedes **potuit**. See note **cui** above.
> **organa…aquarum**: "hydraulic equipment," dir. obj. of **facere**.
> **qui**: logically precedes **organa**. See note **cui** above. Antecedent is **nemo**.
> **no(vi)sset**: "knew how."
> **ducere cursum**: "to lay out a channel."

X. Accusative and Infinitive

85. Remember One Thing (*CIL* 10.7697, 6-7)

QVI · LEGIS · HVNC · TITVLVM · MORTALEM
TE ESSE   MEMENTO

Qui legis hunc titulum, mortalem te esse memento.

From an epitaph found incised into rock at Caralis (modern Cagliari) on the island of Sardinia.

> **titulum**: titulus, -i, m., *inscription.*
> **memento**: imperat. sing. of *memini*: "remember."

86. The Grave of a Poor Man (*CIL* 9.5659, 3-5)

PAVPER · FVIT · AEQVO
ANIMO · SCIBAT · MORIVN
DVM · SIBI

Pauper fuit aequo animo. Sci<e>bat moriendum sibi.

A gravestone found at Treia in Italy. If one accepts the inevitability of death with equanimity—the word we get in English from this combination of *aequus* and *animus*—what is his state of mind?

> **pauper:** pauper, -eris, m., *a poor man.*
> **aequo:** aequus, -a, -um, *equal, even, level, fair, calm.*
> **moriendum:** morior, mori, mortuus sum, *to die.* Supply **esse.**

87. No Reason to Live (*ICUR* 2.4233, 9-10)

VIVERE ME CERTE LIBVIT DVM VIVERIS IPSA
SED MODO MORTE TVA MORS MIHI SOLA PLACET

Vivere me certe libuit dum viver*e*s ipsa,
sed modo morte tuā mors mihi sola placet.

From a grave inscription known from a manuscript at the Vatican, in which a girl is praised by her mother. See also **26** and **116**.

> **certe:** adv., *certainly.*
> **libuit:** libet, libēre, libuit or libitum est, impersonal verb, *it pleases, it is agreeable.* Governs an accusative and infinitive construction here.
> **dum viver*e*s:** "while you were alive." The spelling **viveris** is almost certainly a composer's or engraver's error. Emending to **viveres** seems to be the best solution, even if this yields an unclassical construction after **dum.**
> **ipsa:** fem. nom. sing. of ipse, ipsa, ipsum, intensive pron., *myself, yourself, himself, herself, itself.*
> **modo:** "now."

88. Poor Wall (*CIL* 4.2487; Courtney 77; Wallace II.185)

A DMIROR TII PARIES· NON CECIDISSE
QVI TOT·SCR IPTORVM·TAEDIA· SVSTINEAS

AD · MIROR TE · PARIES · NON C[E]CIDISSE
QVI TOT · SCRIPTORVM TAEDIA SVSTINEAS

———◆———

**Admiror te, paries, non cecidisse qui tot scriptorum
taedia sustineas.**

———◆———

A graffito found at the Amphitheatre in Pompeii. The same witticism appears, in a slightly different form, near the forum on the other side of town. The verb *sustineo* is here used in two senses: the wall must not only put up with all the graffiti upon it, but literally support their weight as well.

admiror: admiror, -ari, admiratus sum, *to admire, be astonished at, wonder.*

paries: paries, -ietis, m., *wall.*

c[e]cidisse: cado, cadere, cecidi, *to fall, fall down; collapse.*

tot: adv., *so many.*

scriptorum: scriptor, -oris, m., *writer.*

taedia: taedium, -i, n., *a nuisance, tedium.* Translate: "tedious scribblings."

qui...sustineas: "you who bear."

89. A Hope Unrealized (*CIL* 6.9659, 1-7)

L · LICINIVS
M · F · POL · NEPOS ·
CVIVS · DE · VITA · MERITO
POTE · NEMO · QVERI
QVI · NEGOTIANDO · LOCVPLETEM
SE · SPERAVIT · ESSE · FVTVRVM
SPE · DECEPTVS · ERAT

L(ucius) Licinius M(arci) f(ilius) Pol(lia) Nepos,
cuius de vita merito pote<st> nemo queri, qui
negotiando locupletem se speravit esse futurum, spe
deceptus erat.

From a gravestone found in Rome.

> **L(ucius) Licinius...Nepos:** *Lucius Licinius Nepos.* Antecedent of both
>   **cuius** and **qui.**
> **Pol(lia):** "of the voting-tribe Pollia."
> **merito:** "rightly."
> **queri:** queror, queri, questus sum, *to complain.*
> **negotiando:** "by conducting business."
> **locupletem:** locuples, -pletis, *rich.* Predicate of the infinitive **esse**
>   **futurum.**
> **se:** Subj. of the infinitive **esse futurum.**
> **esse futurum:** i.e., **futurum esse,** fut. act. infin. of sum, *to be.*
> **deceptus:** decipio, -cipere, -cepi, -ceptum, *to catch, deceive, foil, cheat.*

XI.   Participles

90. Inconsolable (*CIL* 6.25808, 5-6)

RELIQVISTI MAMMAM TVAM
GEMENTEM · PLANGENTEM · PLORANTEM

Reliquisti mammam tuam gementem, plangentem,
plorantem.

From an epitaph found in Rome. The words are addressed by a mother to her
daughter, Salvidiena Faustilla, who lived "15 years, 3 months, 11 days and 7
hours." What effect does this precision have on the reader of the epitaph? (For

a less precisely calculated lifespan, see **73**). The composer of this epitaph is versed in the tools of rhetoric. The similarity of endings ("homeoteleuton") and the absence of any connecting word such as "and" ("asyndeton") add emotion and power to the participles *gementem, plangentem, plorantem,* which are themselves arranged in a group of three ("tricolon").

gementem: gemo, gemere, gemui, gemitum, *to sigh, lament.*
plangentem: plango, plangere, planxi, planctum, *to wail, bewail.*
plorantem: ploro, -are, -avi, -atum, *to cry aloud in grief, to weep over.*

91. Devotion (*CIL* 13.3081, 3-7)

**AMANS AMAN
TI HAEC TIBI
PRO MERITIS
DO
CARATVS**

Amans amanti haec tibi pro meritis do Caratus.

From a gravestone found at Caesarodunum (Tours, France). What effect does the juxtaposition of *amans* and *amanti* have on the reader of the epitaph? What words in the epitaph do these participles modify?

meritis: meritum, -i, n., *desert, merit.*
Caratus: Caratus, -i, m., *Caratus.*

92. Only Ashes (*CIL* 6.7419, 1)

FVMANTES · ITERVM · CINERES · QVID · RESPICIS · HOSPES

Fumantes iterum cineres quid respicis, hospes?

From an epitaph inscribed on a black marble tablet found in Rome. What is the effect of this rhetorical question?

fumantes: fumo, fumare, fumavi, *to smoke, steam.*
iterum: iterum, adv., *again, a second time.*
quid: "why?"
respicis: respicio, -spicere, -spexi, -spectum, *to look back.*
hospes: hospes, hospitis, m., *guest, host, stranger, passerby.*

93. One Small Request (*CIL* 2.558, 5-9)

**TV QVI CARPIS ITER GRESSV
PROPERANTE VIATOR SISTE
GRADV QVAESO QVOD PETO PARVA
MORA EST ORO VT PRAETERIENS
DICAS · S · T · T · L**

**Tu qui carpis iter gressu properante, viator, siste
gradu<m>, quaeso. Quod peto, parva mora est: oro
ut praeteriens dicas, "s(it) t(erra) t(ibi) l(evis)."**

A gravestone found at Emerita Augusta (Mérida, Spain). The common formula
S.T.T.L. ("May the earth be light upon you") could be interpreted as implying a
literal belief in a sensate corpse, but should probably be interpreted in a looser,
more poetic sense. See also **109, 124** and **125**.

> **carpis**: carpo, carpere, carpsi, carptum, *to seize, pluck*; (with **iter**) *to
>   proceed, make one's way.*
> **gressu**: gressus, -us, m., *step, course.*
> **properante**: propero, -are, -avi, -atum, *to hasten, hurry.*
> **siste**: sisto, sistere, stiti, statum, *to stop, halt* (transitive).
> **gradu<m>**: gradus, -us, m., *step, pace.*
> **quaeso**: quaeso, quaesere, *to beg, entreat.*
> **peto**: peto, petere, petivi, petitum, *to seek, ask for; aim for, emulate.*
> **parva**: parvus, -a, -um, *small.*
> **ut...dicas**: "that you say."
> **praeteriens**: praetereo, -ire, -ii, -itum, *to go past, pass by.*
> **s(it) t(erra) t(ibi) l(evis)**: "May the earth be light upon you."

94. Dedication to Mithras (*RIB* 4)

**[DEO MITHRAE ET SOLI] INVICTO
[AB ORIENTE] AD
[OCCID]ENTEM**

Deo Mithrae et soli invicto ab oriente ad occidentem.

Part of an inscribed marble panel found in a Temple to Mithras in Londinium
(London, England). Mithras, a Persian deity associated with the sun and often
represented in the act of slaying a bull, inspired a cult that attracted numerous
adherents throughout the Roman Empire beginning in the first century AD.

Open only to men, the cult was particularly popular with Roman soldiers. Confident restoration of the fragmentary inscription above is made possible by comparison with similar inscriptions that have been found.

Mithrae: Mithras, -ae, m., *Mithras*.
soli: sol, solis, m., *sun*.
invicto: invictus, -a, -um, *unconquered*.
oriente: orior, oriri, ortus sum, *to rise*.
occidentem: occido, -ere, -cidi, -casum, *to fall*; (of the sun) *to set*.

95. A Sacred Spot Restored (*RIB* 152)

LOCVM RELIGIOSVM
PER INSOLENTIAM
ERVTVM
VIRTVT ET N
AVG REPVRGATVM
REDDIDIT
C SEVERIVS
EMERITVS C
REG

Locum religiosum per insolentiam erutum, virtut(i)
et n(umini) Aug(usti) repurgatum, reddidit G(aius)
Severius emeritus c(enturio) reg(ionis).

Inscription found at Aquae Sulis (Bath, England), recording the restoration of a sacred spot by Gaius Severius, a veteran centurion in the Roman army. The divinity concerned, the *Numen Augusti*, is the "living divinity" or "divine spirit" of the reigning emperor, and does not refer to Augustus himself. For the title *Augustus* designating any emperor, see **118**.

insolentiam: insolentia, -ae, f., *insolence, arrogance*.
erutum: eruo, -ere, -ui, -utum, *to destroy, demolish*.
n(umini): numen, -inis, n., *divinity, divine spirit, living spirit*.
Aug(usti): Augustus, -i, m., *Augustus*, a name granted to Octavian in 27 BC, and then to every subsequent Roman emperor.
repurgatum: repurgo, -are, -avi, -atum, *to clean or clean afresh*.
reddidit: reddo, reddere, reddidi, redditum, *to restore*.
G(aius) Severius: *Gaius Severius*.
emeritus: emeritus, -a, -um, *veteran, retired*.
c(enturio): centurio, -onis, m., *a centurion*. The "C" on the stone is actually inscribed in reverse.
reg(ionis): regio, -ionis, f., *region, district*.

96. Among the Stars (*ICUR* 8.20798)

PRAESBYTER HIC SITVS EST CELERINVS NOMINE DIC[TVS]
CORPOREOS RVMPENS NEXVS QVI GAVDET IN ASTRIS

Presbyter hīc situs est Celerinus nomine dictus,
corporeos rumpens nexus qui gaudet in astris.

A gravestone, located in the Church of St. Agnes on the *Via Nomentana* outside
Rome, commemorating a priest named Celerinus. Datable to AD 381 because of
an additional inscription on the stone noting that it was laid in the consulship
of Syagrius and Eucerius. What conception of the body and soul is implied by
this sentiment? What conception of the afterlife?

> **presbyter**: presbyter, -teri, m., *priest.*
> **Celerinus**: Celerinus, -i, m., *Celerinus.*
> **corporeos**: corporeus, -a, -um, *bodily, corporeal.*
> **rumpens**: rumpo, rumpere, rupi, ruptum, *to burst open, break through.*
> **nexus**: nexus, -us, m., *a binding; restraint.*

97. When He Comes (*CIL* 12.2111, 5-6)

SVRRC · DIE CAELO · CVM
VENERIT AVCTOR

Surr(e)c(turus) die caelo cum venerit auctor

From an epitaph inscribed on a marble tablet found in the Roman town of
Vienna (Vienne, France). Beneath the text are pictured two creatures which,
it has been suggested, are meant to represent phoenixes, the mythical birds
that rose from their own ashes. What view of the afterlife is implied by this
sentiment?

> **surr(e)c(turus)**: surgo, surgere, surrexi, surrectum, *to rise up.*
> **cum**: "when."
> **auctor**: auctor, -oris, m., *originator, author; creator.*

98. Weep for Me (*CIL* 5.6714, 12-13)

LACRIMAS · TITVLO · NOLI
MORITVRE · NEGARE

Lacrimas titulo noli, moriture, negare.

From an epitaph found in Vercellae (Vercelli, Italy). Why does the deceased address the reader as *moriture*, and how does this relate to what he asks of him?

lacrimas: lacrima, -ae, f., *tear.*
titulo: titulus, -i, m., *inscription.*
moriture: fut. act. participle of morior, mori, mortuus sum, *to die.*

XII.   Ablative Absolute

99. Immortality! (*CIL* 1².2997; 6.30157)

CORPORE · CONSVMPT[O] VIVA · ANIMA · DEVS · SVM

Corpore consumpto, vivā animā, deus sum.

From an epitaph inscribed on a Travertine slab found in Rome, which, judging by its lettering, seems to date at least as far back as the period of Augustus. What conception of the body and soul are implied by this sentiment?

consumpto: consumo, -sumere, -sumpsi, -sumptum, *to consume, waste away, destroy.*
vivā: vivus, -a, -um, *living, alive.*

100. Octavian: Savior of the Republic (*CIL* 6.873)

> **SENATVS · POPVLVSQVE · ROMANVS**
> **IMP · CAESARI · DIVI · IVLI · F · COS · QVINCT**
> **COS · DESIGN · SEXT · IMP · SEPT**
> **REPVBLICA · CONSERVATA**

> **Senatus populusque Romanus imp(eratori) Caesari,**
> **divi Iuli f(ilio), co(n)s(uli) quinct(um), co(n)s(uli)**
> **design(ato) sext(um), imp(eratori) sept(imum),**
> **republicā conservatā.**

Inscription on a nine foot block of marble found in the Roman Forum, and thought to be from the Arch of Augustus, dedicated in 29 BC to commemorate his victory over Antony at the battle of Actium. Following this event, Octavian, who would not be granted the title "Augustus" until 27 BC, found himself in a position of unparalleled power in Rome. But note the care with which his message is crafted: Octavian's victory over Antony marks not the accession to power by one man, but the preservation of the Republic (*republica conservata*).

> **imp(eratori)**: imperator, -oris, m., *leader, commander.* (Only later does this word gather the associations of "emperor.")
>
> **Caesari**: refers here to Octavian, who assumes the name of his adoptive father Julius Caesar.
>
> **divi Iuli**: refers to Julius Caesar, who was deified after his death.
>
> **quinct(um)**: quinctum (also spelled quintum), adv., *for the fifth time.*
>
> **design(ato)**: designatus, -a, -um, *elected, designate* (but not yet in office).
>
> **sext(um)**: sextum, adv., *for the sixth time.*
>
> **sept(imum)**: septimum, adv., *for the seventh time.*
>
> **conservatā**: conservo, -are, -avi, -atum, *to keep, preserve.*

101. Ball-player (*CIL* 6.9797, 1-6; Courtney 124)

VRSVS TOGATVS VITREA QVI PRIMVS PILA
LVSI DECENTER CVM MEIS LVSORIBVS
LAVDANTE POPVLO MAXIMIS CLAMORIBVS
THERMIS TRAI{I}ANI THERMIS AGRIPPAE ET TITI
MVLTVM ET NERONIS SI TAMEN MIHI CREDITIS
EGO SVM

Ursus togatus vitreā qui primus pilā lusi decenter cum
meis lusoribus laudante populo maximis clamoribus
thermis Traiani, thermis Agrippae et Titi, multum et
Neronis, si tamen mihi creditis, ego sum.

From an epitaph inscribed on a large marble tablet found in Rome, now in the Vatican. Although it appears at first glance to involve a toga-wearing bear (ursus, -i, m., *bear*), this inscription concerns a man named Ursus who made his living performing with a glass ball in various public baths in Rome. Public baths played an integral role in Roman life, not only providing facilities for bathing (many homes and apartments did not have plumbing), but also serving as centers of recreation, exercise, education, entertainment, and general socializing. On the variety of activities that went on in a public bath building, see Seneca, *Letters* 56.1-2, where he complains about the noise reaching his upstairs apartment. What Ursus was doing with the ball is not entirely clear, but the significance of its being made of glass must be that it would shatter if dropped.

Ursus: Ursus, -i, m., *Ursus* (predicate of **sum**, line 6).

togatus: togatus, -i, m., *Roman citizen*. Substantive from togatus, -a, -um, *toga-clad*. The idea seems to be not that Ursus was the first to do this, but the first Roman citizen (Courtney).

vitreā: vitreus, -a, -um, *glass, made of glass*. To be translated after the relative pronoun **qui**.

pilā: pila, -ae, f., *ball*.

decenter: decenter, adv., *properly, pleasingly, gracefully*.

lusoribus: lusor, -oris, m., *player*.

maximis: maximus, -a, -um, *the greatest*.

thermis: thermae, -arum, f., *baths* (ablative of place where, without a preposition).

Traiani: Traianus, -i, m., *Trajan*, Roman emperor AD 98-117.

Agrippae: Agrippa, -ae, m., *Agrippa*, close friend and supporter of Augustus, responsible for the building of the Pantheon, as well as the baths described here, the first great bathing complex in Rome (25 BC).

Titi: Titus, -i, m., *Titus*, Roman Emperor AD 79-81.

multum: "much" or "often."

Neronis: Nero, Neronis, m., *Nero*, Roman emperor AD 54-68.

102. Mummius: Destroyer of Corinth (*CIL* 1².626; 6.331; Courtney 3; Gordon 11)

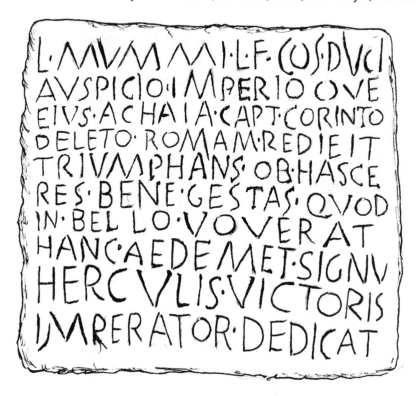

L · MVMMI · L · F · COS · DVCT
AVSPICIO · IMPERIOQVE
EIVS · ACHAIA · CAPT · CORINTO
DELETO · ROMAM · REDI{E}IT
TRIVMPHANS · OB · HASCE
RES · BENE · GESTAS · QVOD
IN · BELLO · VOVERAT
HANC · AEDEM · ET · SIGNV
HERCVLIS · VICTORIS
IMPERATOR · DEDICAT

L(ucius) Mummi(us) L(uci) f(ilius) co(n)s(ul). Duct(u),
auspicio imperioque eius Achaea capt(a est). Corint\<h\>o
deleto Romam rediit triumphans. Ob hasce res bene
gestas, quod in bello voverat, hanc aedem et signu(m)
Herculis Victoris, imperator dedicat.

A dedicatory inscription found on the Caelian Hill in Rome. In 146 BC the army of general Lucius Mummius captured and destroyed the Greek city of Corinth, an event significant not only for the unusual degree of brutality exhibited by the Romans, but because it marked the official annexation of Greece into the growing Roman Empire. The inscription above records a dedication by Mummius commemorating his achievement.

L(ucius)...co(n)s(ul): The syntax is clearest if these words are understood as standing alone, without a verb: "Lucius Mummius, son of Lucius, consul."

duct(u): ductus, -us, m., *command, leadership.*

auspicio: auspicium, -i, n., *command, guidance, auspices.*

Achaia: Achaia, -ae, f., *Achaia,* the Romans' name for the province they established in southern Greece.

Corint<h>o: Corinthus, -i, f. (but m. here), *Corinth.*

deleto: deleo, -ēre, -evi, -etum, *to destroy.*

rediit: redeo, -ire, -ivi and -ii, -itum, *to return.*

triumphans: triumpho, -are, -avi, -atum, *to triumph, to celebrate a triumph.*

hasce: "these," fem. acc. plur.

gestas: gero, gerere, gessi, gestum, *to wage, do, accomplish, carry out.*

quod: "that which," dir. obj. of *voverat,* referring to **hanc aedem et signu(m) Herculis Victoris.**

voverat: voveo, vovēre, vovi, votum, *to vow, promise.*

aedem: aedes, aedis, f., *rooms, house; temple.*

signu(m): signum, -i, n., *sign, signal; statue.*

103. Pompey the Great (Pliny *Natural History* 7.97)

**Gn(aeus) Pompeius Magnus imperator, bello
XXX annorum confecto, fusis fugatis occisis in
deditionem acceptis hominum centiens viciens
semel LXXXIII, depressis aut captis navibus
DCCCXLVI, oppidis castellis MDXXXVIII in
fidem receptis, terris a Maeotis ad Rubrum Mare
subactis, votum merito Minervae.**

An inscription reported by Pliny the Elder (*Natural History* 7.97), recording the achievements of Pompey the Great during his eastern campaigns (66-62 BC). The inscription is said to have been belonged to a shrine dedicated by Pompey to Minerva upon his return. While we cannot be certain that Pliny's text reports the exact wording of the inscription, it does accurately reflect the Romans' propensity for citing the achievements of emperors and generals with strings of successive ablative absolutes.

> **Gn(aeus) Pompeius Magnus**: Gnaeus Pompeius Magnus, better known
>   as Pompey the Great.
> **fusis**: fundo, fundere, fudi, fusum, *to rout, scatter.*
> **fugatis**: fugo, -are, -avi, -atum, *to put to flight.*
> **occisis**: occido, occidere, occidi, occisum, *to kill.*
> **deditionem**: deditio, -ionis, f., *surrender*
> **centiens viciens semel LXXXIII**: 2,183,000.
> **depressis**: deprimo, -primere, -pressi, -pressum, *to sink* (transitive).
> **oppidis**: oppidum, -i, n., *town.*
> **castellis**: castellum, -i, n., *fortress.*
> **receptis**: recipio, -cipere, -cepi, -ceptum, *receive, accept, take.*
> **a Maeotis ad Rubrum Mare**: "from the Sea of Azov to the Red Sea."
> **subactis**: subigo, -igere, -egi, -actum, *to subdue.*
> **votum**: votum, -i, n., *vow, promise.* Direct object of an implied verb
>   "fulfilled."
> **merito**: "rightly."
> **Minervae**: Minerva, -ae, f., *Minerva.*

XIII.   Comparative and Superlative

104. The End (*CIL* 5.4654, 5-6)

VLTERIVS · NIHIL · EST
MORTE · NEQVE · VTILIVS

Ulterius nihil est morte neque utilius.

Inscribed on a gravestone found at Brixia (Breschia, Italy). What view of death is implied by this sentiment?

> **ulterius**: compar. of ultro, *far off, remote*.
> **utilius**: compar. of utilis, -e, *useful, beneficial*.

105. My Sweet (*CIL* 6.19055, 1-2)

HOC · IACET · IN TVMVLO · SECVRA · GLYCONIS · HONESTO
DVLCIS · NOMINE ERAT ANIMA QVOQVE DVLCIOR · VSQVE

Hōc iacet in tumulo secura Glyconis honesto.
Dulcis nomine erat, animā quoque dulcior usque.

From a gravestone in the Capitoline Museum, Rome. The composer makes a pun on Glyconis's name, which sounds like it comes from the Greek word γλυκύς, *sweet*. The composer was careful in his arrangement of words. In the sequence *tumulo secura Glyconis honesto*, *honesto* goes with *tumulo* (both abl. sing.) and *secura* with *Glyconis* (both nom. sing.). This arrangement into an ABBA pattern is known as "chiasmus," from the Greek letter *chi* (X), the shape generated by connecting the corresponding elements:

tumulo   secura

Glyconis   honesto

Now look again at the Latin as it appears on the stone. What mental picture is generated in this epitaph by the nesting of *secura Glyconis* between *tumulo* and *honesto*?

> **tumulo**: tumulus, -i, m., *mound, tomb*.
> **secura**: securus, -a, -um, *untroubled, released from care, composed*.
> **Glyconis**: *Glyconis*, nominative singular.
> **honesto**: honestus, -a, -um, *honorable, respectable, distinguished*.
> **usque**: adv., *even*.

106. The Cruel Sisters (*CIL* 3.9259, 4-5)

**[QV]OD SI LONGA MAGIS DVXISSENT FILA SORORES · AEQVIVS IS
[TE L]APIS COMPLECTERET OSSA PATERNA**

**Quod si longa magis duxissent fila sorores,
aequius iste lapis complecteret ossa paterna.**

From a gravestone found at Salona (Solin, Croatia). The sisters mentioned are the
three Fates (*Parcae*), who spun, measured and cut the thread of life allotted to
each mortal. The unnaturalness of parents burying their children is a common
theme in Latin epitaphs. See also **140**.

quod: "but."

si...duxissent: "if (they) had drawn out," with **fila** as dir. obj.

longa magis: equivalent to **longiora**. The word magis ("more") is often
used with adjectives that have no regular comparative form, but is
unusual with a word like longus.

fila: filum, -i, n., *thread.*

iste: masc. nom. sing. of iste, ista, istud, *that...of yours.*

lapis: lapis, lapidis, m., *stone.*

complecteret: "would embrace."

ossa: os, ossis, n., *bone.*

107. To Our Son (*CIL* 6.16010)

DIS · MAN
COMICVS · ET
AVRIOLA · PARENTES
INFELICISSIMI
P · LICINIO · SVCCESSO
V · A · XIII · M · I · D · XIX

Dis Man(ibus). Comicus et Auriola, parentes
infelicissimi, P(ublio) Licinio Successo. V(ixit)
a(nnos) XIII, m(enses) I, d(ies) XIX.

Inscription on a funerary altar found in a vineyard in Rome, now in the British Museum. A simple epitaph addressed to Publius Licinius Successus by his parents. Other than the standard elements—invocation of the Departed Spirits, name of deceased and his lifespan, names of those responsible for the monument—the inscription bears a single non-essential word, *infelicissimi*. What is the effect of this word on the reader of the epitaph?

Comicus: Comicus, -i, m., *Comicus*.
Auriola: Auriola, -ae, f., *Auriola*.
infelicissimi: infelix, -icis, *unlucky, woeful; unhappy, miserable*.
P(ublio) Licinio Successo: *Publius Licinius Successus*.

108. Dearest Wife? (*CIL* 6.29149)

D · M
M · VLPIVS · CERDO
TITVLVM · POSVIT
CLAVDIAE · TYCHENI
CONIVGI · KARISSIM
CVM QVA · VIX · ANNIS
II · MENS VI · DIEB ·
III · HOR · X· IN DIE
MORTIS · GRATIAS
MAXIMAS · EGI
APVT · DEOS · ET
APVT · HOMINES

D(is) M(anibus). M(arcus) Ulpius Cerdo titulum posuit Claudiae Tycheni, coniugi *c*arissim(ae), cum quā vix(it) annis II, mensibus VI, dieb(us) III, hor(is) X. In die mortis *g*ratias maximas egi<t> apu*d* deos et apu*d* homines.

Epitaph inscribed on a marble tablet found in Rome, now in the British Museum, commissioned by Marcus Ulpius Cerdo for his wife Claudia Tyche. The language and thought are unremarkable until one reaches *in die mortis gratias maximas egit*, which seems to mean "on the day of her death he gave the greatest thanks"—an implausibly sardonic remark for a Roman tombstone, particularly when juxtaposed with *carissimae*. One must either suppose that the inscribed text represents *in die<u>m</u> mortis*, "until the day of her death," with the final consonant suppressed (as often in Latin inscriptions), or that the sense of the inscribed text is something like "on the day of her death he gave the greatest thanks *that he was able to spend what time he had with her.*"

M(arcus) Ulpius Cerdo: *Marcus Ulpius Cerdo.*
titulum: titulus, -i, m., *inscription.*
Claudiae Tycheni: *Claudia Tyche.*
coniugi: coniunx, coniugi, c., *spouse.*
annis...mensibus...dieb(us)...hor(is): occasionally in later Latin the ablative, not the accusative, is used to express duration of time. See also **73**.
in die mortis: see introductory note.

109. Too Young (*CIL* 6.22321, 2-7)

MAXIMVS · HIC · RECVBO
DVLCISSIMVS · INFAS · BIMVLVS
IN TERTIVM ESCENDENS SIS ·
MIHI TERRA LEVIS · DVLCIS ·
ERAM · MATRI · CARIOR
VSQVE PATRI

**Maximus hīc recubo dulcissimus infa<n>s bimulus
in tertium escendens. Sis mihi, terra, levis. Dulcis
eram matri, carior usque patri.**

Epitaph inscribed on a marble tablet in the Capitoline Museum in Rome. The deceased, a boy named Maximus, speaks the lines above, which happen to contain examples of all three degrees of the adjective—not including his name, which is itself the superlative degree of *magnus*!

> **Maximus**: Maximus, -i, m., *Maximus*.
> **recubo**: recubo, -are, -avi, -atum, *to lie, repose*.
> **bimulus**: bimulus, -a, -um, *two years old*.
> **tertium**: i.e., **tertium annum**.
> **escendens**: escendo, -scendere, -scendi, -scensum, *to ascend, advance, approach*.
> **Sis mihi, terra, levis**: "Earth, may you be light upon me."
> **usque**: adv., *even*.

XIV.   Gerund, Gerundive, and Passive Periphrastic

110. Bad to Worse (*CIL* 4.1870; Wallace II.174)

MINIMVM · MALVM · FIT CONTEMNENDO · MAXVMVM ·
MENEDEMERVMENVS

Minimum malum fit contemnendo max*i*mum.

A graffito from Pompeii. The same thought is also found scratched on a wall in Herculaneum. The Romans were fond of such pithy maxims, a mode of expression well suited to the concision of Latin. The meaning, if any, of the sequence MENEDEMERVMENVS is uncertain, although it may be a reference to a comedy by Terence called *Heautontimorumenos* ("The Self-Tormentor"), which features a character named Menedemus.

> **fit**: fio, fieri, factus sum, *to become, be made*.
> **contemnendo**: contemno, -temnere, -tempsi, -temptum, *to despise, disdain, neglect*. Understand "it" as dir. obj.

111. To Urbanilla (*CIL* 8.152, 5-6)

NVLLA SPES VIVENDI MIHI SINE · CONIVGE · TALI · ILLA DOMVM SERVARE MEAM ILLA ET CONSILIO IVVARE

Nulla spes vivendi mihi sine coniuge tali:
Illa domum servare meam, illa et consilio iuvare.

From an epitaph found near Thelepte (Tunisia), dating to the end of the 2nd or beginning of the 3rd century AD. Elsewhere in the inscription, the deceased Urbanilla is described by her husband not only as a careful manager of their household, but as a shrewd business partner outside the home (*comes negotiorum*). In addition, the inscription forms an acrostic, with the first letters of each line spelling V R B A N I L L A down the left side of the stone (only the N and I are represented here). Her husband is to be understood as speaking the lines above.

> **coniuge**: coniunx, -iugis, c., *spouse*.
> **tali**: talis, tale, *such, of such a kind*.
> **servare**: servo, -are, -avi, -atum, *to keep; watch over*. Historical infinitive. Translate: "she kept."
> **iuvare**: iuvo, -are, iuvi, iutum, *to help*. Historical infinitive. Translate: "she helped (me)."

112. The Good Die Young (*CIL* 12.592, 23-24)

LVGEMVS · TE · MISERANDE · PVER QVIA · BREVE · OMNE · QVOD BONVM · EST

Lugemus te, miserande puer, quia breve omne quod
bonum est.

From an epitaph inscribed on a marble tablet found at Aquae Sextiae (Aix-en-Provence, France). The words are addressed to the deceased.

> **lugemus**: lugeo, lugēre, luxi, *to mourn*.
> **miserande**: miseror, miserari, miseratus sum, *to pity*.
> **breve**: predicate (with understood **est**) of **omne**.

113. One Home (*CIL* 6.25617, 11)

VNA · DOMVS · CVNCTIS · NEC · FVGIENDA · VIRIS

Una domus cunctis nec fugienda viris.

From an epitaph found in Rome. For the idea of death as the common destination of all mortals, see **142** and **143**.

    una domus: supply **est**.
    cunctis: cunctus, -a, -um, *all*.
    fugienda: fugio, fugere, fugi, fugitum, *to flee, escape, avoid.*

114. Fabrician Bridge (*CIL* 6.1305; Gordon 18; Keppie, p. 63)

**L · FABRICIVS · C · F · CVR · VIAR
FACIVNDVM · COERAVIT**

**L(ucius) Fabricius G(ai) f(ilius) cur(ator) viar(um)
faciendum curavit.**

Main inscription from the Fabrician Bridge in Rome. Originally build in 62 BC, the year after Cicero's consulship, the bridge still spans the Tiber River from the left bank to Tiber Island.

    L(ucius) Fabricius: *Lucius Fabricius.*
    G(ai): Gaius, -i, m., *Gaius.*
    cur(ator): curator, -oris, m., *overseer, superintendent.*
    curavit: curo, -are, -avi, -atum, *to take care of, see to, manage.*

115. Portico at Pompeii (*CIL* 1².1627; 10.794)

V · POPIDIVS
EP · F · Q ·
PORTICVS
FACIENDAS
[C]OERAVIT

**V(ibius) Popidius Ep(idii) f(ilius) q(uaestor) porticus
faciendas curavit.**

Inscription found at Pompeii, recording the construction of porticos (colonnades)
around the forum. The Popidius clan was one with a long history at Pompeii (see
also **145**).

V(ibius) Popidius: *Vibius Popidius.*
Ep(idii): Epidius, -i, m., *Epidius.*
q(uaestor): quaestor, -oris, m., *quaestor,* an elected position in Roman
 government concerned with the supervision of the treasury.
porticus: porticus, -us, f., *portico, colonnade.*

116. Who Could Believe? (*ICUR* 2.4233, 7)

ADMIRANDA LOQVOR QVIS AVTEM CREDERE POSSIT

Admiranda loquor, quis autem credere possit?

From a grave inscription known from a manuscript at the Vatican, in which a
girl is praised by her mother. See also **26** and **87**. What is the implied answer to
the rhetorical question?

admiranda: admiror, -ari, admiratus sum, *to admire, be astonished at,
 wonder.*
loquor: loquor, loqui, locutus sum, *to say, speak.*
quis: quis, quid, *who?, what?; why?*
credere: credo, credere, credidi, creditum, *to believe* (+ dat.). Understand
 an unexpressed **mihi** as object.
possit: "could," 3rd pers. sing. pres. subjunctive of possum, *to be able.*

117. Don't Be Sad (*CIL* 6.11592, 6-7)

NOLI DO[L]E[RE] MAMMA
FACIENDVM FVIT

Noli dolere, mamma; faciendum fuit.

From a tablet marking a niche for funerary ashes, found in Rome. In this inscription, Ampliata, just four and a half years old, explains the inevitability of death to her mother, adding, "my time was over quickly, because my fate wanted it so."

PART 4

The Syntax of the Subjunctive Mood

XV. Hortatory/Jussive

118. A Reasonable Request (*CIL* 6.3413, 6-7)

NE QVIS HIC VRINA
FACIAT

Ne quis hīc urina\<m> faciat.

From an epitaph inscribed on a marble tablet found in Rome, now in the Vatican Museum. The preceding part of the inscription identifies the commissioner of the inscription as a member of the *Evocati Augusti*, that is, a distinguished soldier in the emperor's Praetorian Guard who has discharged his service and then been recalled to duty. As often, the use of the name *Augustus* here refers not to Augustus himself, but to the reigning emperor (see also **95**). In the lines above, this soldier warns against defiling his grave.

    quis: aliquis, aliquid, *someone, something, anyone, anything.*
    urina\<m>: urina, -ae, f., *urine.*

119. In Praise of Love (*CIL* 4.4091; Courtney 88; Wallace II.129)

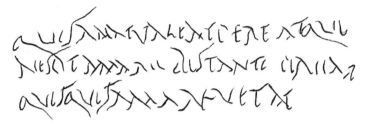

**QVIS AMAT VALEAT PEREAT QVI
NESCIT AMARE BIS TANTO PEREAT
QVISQVIS AMARE VETAT**

**<Quis>quis amat, valeat; pereat, qui nescit amare;
bis tanto pereat quisquis amare vetat.**

A graffito from Pompeii. The same idea and adaptations of it recur a number of times throughout the city. Note the chiasmus (for definition, see **105**) in *quis amat valeat pereat qui nescit*, which achieves a striking effect by placing side by side two hortatory subjunctives with antithetical meanings: *valeat* and *pereat*.

<quis>quis: quisquis, quidquid, *whoever, whichever, whatever.*
valeat: valeo, -ēre, -ui, -itum, *to be well.*
pereat: pereo, -ire, -ivi and -ii, -itum, *to perish, die.*
bis tanto: "twice more again."
vetat: veto, -are, vetui, vetitum, *to forbid, prevent, outlaw.*

120. Not Here (*CIL* 6.29848b)

**DVODECIM DEOS ET DEANAM ET IOVEM
OPTVMVM MAXIMV · HABEAT IRATOS
QVISQVIS HIC MIXERIT AVT CACARIT**

**Duodecim deos et Dianam et Iovem Optimum
Maximu<m> habeat iratos, quisquis hīc mixerit aut
caca(ve)rit.**

Found painted on a plaster wall at the site of the Baths of Titus in Rome, above a representation of two snakes. The snakes represent the *genius loci*, the protective spirit of the place, which would be offended by any urination or defecation in its vicinity. For the *genius loci*, see also **21**. The "twelve gods" refers to the chief deities worshipped by the Romans, sometimes referred to as the *Dii Consentes*: Jupiter, Juno, Neptune, Minerva, Apollo, Diana, Mars, Venus, Vulcan, Vesta, Mercury and Ceres. In the lines above the subject of *habeat* is defined by the relative clause *quisquis hic mixerit aut cacarit*.

> **et...et**: since Diana and Jupiter are already included in the twelve, this should be translated "especially...and."
> **Dianam**: Diana, -ae, f., *Diana*.
> **Iovem**: Iuppiter, Iovis, m., *Jupiter*.
> **Optimum Maximu<m>**: a common epithet of Jupiter.
> **iratos**: iratus, -a, -um, *angry*. Here, used as a predicate: "let him have the twelve gods, etc...angry (at him)."
> **quisquis**: quisquis, quidquid, *whoever, whichever, whatever*.
> **mixerit**: mingo, mingere, minxi or mixi, mictum, *to urinate*.
> **caca(ve)rit**: caco, -are, -avi, -atum, *to defecate*.

121. Threat of Blindness (*CIL* Suppl. Ital. 1, n. 633)

**STERCVS INTRA
CIPPOS QVI FECERIT
AVT VIOLARIT NE{I}
LVMINIBVS FRVATVR**

**Stercus intra cippos qui fecerit aut violarit, ne
luminibus fruatur.**

Inscription found at Verona in Italy, which warns against desecrating a sacred space. The subject of *fruatur* is defined by the relative clause *qui stercus intra cippos fecerit*.

> **stercus**: stercus, -oris, n., *dung, manure*.
> **cippos**: cippus, -i, m., *stake, pillar, gravestone*.
> **luminibus**: lumen, -inis, n., *light; eye*.
> **fruor**: fruor, frui, fructus sum (+ abl.), *to enjoy*.

122. Do Not Touch (*CIL* 1².499; 15.6902)

NͰ·ATIGAS·NON·SVM·TVA·M·SVM

NE · ATIGAS · NON · SVM · TVA · M · SVM

Ne at\<t\>i\<n\>gas. Non sum tua; M(arci) sum.

Incised on an earthenware lamp found on the Esquiline Hill in Rome. An example of a "talking inscription," where the stone or object itself is represented as speaking (see also **43**). The use of the subjunctive here is sometimes identified more precisely as the "subjunctive of prohibition."

at\<t\>i\<n\>gas: attingo, -ere, -tigi, -tactum, *to touch.*

123 Carpe Diem (*CIL* 6.30103, 1-3)

ADESTE AMICI FRVAMVR TEMPVS BONVM
EPVLEMVR LAETI VITA DVM PARVA MANET
BACCHO MADENTES HILARIS SIT CONCORDIA

**Adeste amici, fruamur tempus bonum, epulemur
laeti, vita dum parva manet, Baccho madentes;
hilaris sit concordia.**

From a marble tablet found at Rome. A vivid expression of the popular Epicurean exhortation to enjoy one's days to the fullest, in view of the brevity of life and the nothingness of death. Compare Horace, *Odes* I.11 (the *carpe diem* poem). See also **74-76**.

adeste: imperat. plur. of adsum, adesse, adfui, *to be present, be at hand.*
fruamur: fruor, frui, fructus sum, *to enjoy* (usually + abl., but with acc. dir. obj. here).
epulemur: epulor, epulari, epulatus sum, *to feast.*
dum: "while." Translate before **vita**.
Baccho: Bacchus, -i, m., *Bacchus* or *Dionysus*, or, by metonymy, *wine*. For metonymy, see **13**.
madentes: madeo, madēre, *to be wet, soaked; to be drunk.*
hilaris: hilaris, -e, *cheerful, merry.*
concordia: concordia, -ae, f., *friendship, fellowship.*

XVI.   Optative

124. S.T.T.L. (*CIL* 8.11594, 8-9)

SI · SVNT · MANES ·
SIT TIBI TERRA · LEVIS ·

***

Si sunt manes, sit tibi terra levis.

***

From a gravestone found at Ammaedarae (Haidra, Tunisia). The stone marked the grave of one Gaius Julius Felix, who lived a remarkable 82 years and 7 months. For the common formula S.T.T.L., see inscriptions **93** and **125**.

> **manes**: manes, -ium, m., *shades of the departed, spirits of the dead.*

125. S.T.T.L. and More (*CIL* 8.21031, 10-12)

DIC
ROGO · PRAETERIENS · HOSPES · SIT · T · T ·
LEVIS · ET · MOLITER OSSA · QVIESCNT

***

Dic, rogo, praeteriens hospes, "Sit t(ibi) t(erra)
levis et mol<l>iter ossa quiesc<a>nt."

***

From a gravestone found at Caesarea Mauretania (Cherchell, Algeria). For the formula S.T.T.L., see **93** and **124**.

> **praeteriens**: praetereo, -ire, -ivi and -ii, -itum, *to go past, pass by.*
> **mol<l>iter**: adv., *easily, gently.*
> **ossa**: os, ossis, n., *bone.*
> **quiesc<a>nt**: quiesco, -ere, -evi, -etum, *to rest, repose.*

126. Felix Felix (*CIL* 4.6815; Wallace II.23)

FELICEM AVFIDIVM FELICEM SEMPER DEVS
FACIAT

***

Felicem Aufidium Felicem semper deus faciat.

***

A graffito from Pompeii. While we cannot know for sure, it is tempting to suppose that the author was Aufidius Felix himself.

> **Aufidium Felicem**: *Aufidius Felix.*

127. Bless You (*CIL* 6.13075, 10-11)

**TV QVI · PERLEGES · VIVAS
VALEAS · AMES · AMERIS**

Tu qui perleges, vivas, valeas, ames, ameris.

From an epitaph inscribed on marble tablet found in Rome.

> **perleges**: perlego, -ere, -legi, -lectum, *to read through, read carefully.*
> Understand "this epitaph" as dir. obj.

128. Wishing You Well (*CIL* 6.2335, 2-4)

**DI VOS
BENE · FACIANT · AMICI · ET · VOS · VIATORES ·
HABEATIS · DEOS · PROPITIOS.**

**Di vos bene faciant, amici, et vos, viatores, habeatis
deos propitios.**

From an epitaph inscribed on a marble block found in Rome.

> **propitios**: propitius, -a, -um, *propitious, favorable.*

129. My Love (*CIL* 6.26489, 7)

O VTINAM IVNCTOS LICVISSET AMORE FRVI

O utinam iunctos licuisset amore frui.

From an epitaph recorded in a 15th century manuscript. What does the tense of the subjunctive imply about the fulfillment of the wish?

> **iunctos**: iungo, iungere, iunxi, iunctum, *to join, unite.* Modifies an
> implied "us."
> **licuisset**: licet, licēre, licuit, impersonal, *it is allowed.* Governs an
> accusative and infinitive construction here.

130. Sad Parting (*CIL* 13.2205, 7-8)

VTINAM NOS
FATVS · TEXISSET · VTROSQVE ·

Utinam nos fatus texisset utrosque.

From a gravestone found at Lugdunum (Lyon, France). The rest of the inscription records that the stone was commissioned by a husband for his wife, with whom he lived for 36 years, three months and ten days. With her death, he says, "a long-standing love affair ended." What does the tense of the subjunctive imply about the fulfillment of the wish?

> **texisset**: tego, tegere, texi, tectum, *to cover, bury.*
> **utrosque**: uterque, utraque, utrumque, *each of two, both.*

XVII.   Purpose Clause and Relative Clause of Purpose

131. Sage Advice

VT BENE CACARET VENTREM PALPAVIT SOLON

Ut bene caceret, ventrem palpavit Solon.

From a wall painting in the Baths of the Seven Sages at Ostia. In this irreverent representation of seven famous Greek statesmen and thinkers of the early 6th century, they are imagined dispensing a different sort of wisdom than they were generally known for. See also 150.

> **cacaret:** caco, -are, -avi, -atum, *to defecate.*
> **ventrem:** venter, -tris, m., *stomach, belly.*
> **palpavit:** palpo, -are, -avi, -atum, *to stroke, pat.*
> **Solon:** *Solon*, nom. sing. The great Athenian statesman.

132. Elysian Fields (*CIL* 6.12877, 2-3)

**HI · SANCTE · COLVERE · DEOS · VIXE[REQVE BEATI]
POST · OBITVM · ELYSIOS [VT] POSSENT [VISERE CAMPOS]**

───◦◦◦◦◦───

**Hi sancte coluer*unt* deos vixer*unt*que beati,
post obitum Elysios ut possent visere campos.**

───◦◦◦◦◦───

An epitaph from Rome, known from a manuscript in the Vatican. The Elysian fields, located sometimes at the westernmost limits of the Earth, sometimes in the underworld, were the blissful destination of the Homeric heroes after death. Later, as the text above illustrates, the Elysian Fields were considered attainable by anyone who lived a virtuous life. Contrast this with the sentiments expressed in **74-76** and **123**.

> **sancte**: "solemnly."
> **coluer*unt***: colo, colere, colui, cultum, *to inhabit, cultivate; honor, cherish, worship.*
> **beati**: beatus, -a, -um, *blessed, happy.* Translate as an adverb here.
> **post obitum Elysios**: translate after **ut**.
> **obitum**: obitus, -us, m., *death.*
> **visere**: viso, visere, visi, visum, *to go to see, visit.*

133. Stop Awhile (*CIL* 12.533, 1-2; Courtney 119)

**PAVLO SISTE GRADVM IVVENIS PIE QVAESO VIATOR
VT MEA PER TITVLVM NORIS SIC INVIDA FATA**

───◦◦◦◦◦───

**Paulo siste gradum, iuvenis pie, quaeso, viator,
ut mea per titulum no(ve)ris sic invida fata.**

───◦◦◦◦◦───

From a tombstone found at Aquae Sextiae (Aix-en-Provence, France). See **35** for more details about the deceased, Sextus Julius Felicissimus, a young man known not only for his skill at hunting animals in the arena, but for healing them as well. The opening of his epitaph, cited above, exhorts any young man passing by to stop and learn of his unfortunate fate.

> **paulo**: "a little while."
> **siste**: sisto, sistere, stiti, statum, *to stop, halt* (transitive).
> **gradum**: gradus, -us, m., *step, pace.*
> **iuvenis**: iuvenis, iuvenis, *young.*
> **pie**: pius, -a, -um, *dutiful, patriotic, godly, kind.*
> **quaeso**: quaeso, quaesere, *to beg, entreat.*
> **no(ve)ris**: 2nd pers. sing. perf. act. subjunct. of nosco, noscere, novi, notum, (perfect with present meaning) *to know.*
> **invida**: invidus, -a, -um, *envious, hateful, unfavorable.*

134. Fighting Habits of the British (*Tab. Vind.* 2.164)

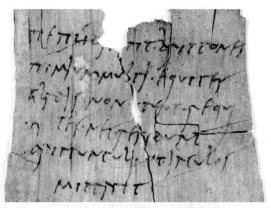

... BRITTONES
NIMIVM MVLTI EQVITES
GLADIS NON VTVNTVR EQVI
TES NEC RESIDVNT
BRITTVNCVLI VT IACVLOS
MITTANT

...Brittones. Nimium multi equites. Gladi<i>s non utuntur
equites nec residunt Brittunculi ut iaculos mittant.

One of hundreds of writing tablets found at Vindolanda, a Roman fort south of Hadrian's Wall in Chesterholm, England. These tablets, consisting of thin, roughly postcard-sized pieces of wood, were written upon with ink and usually then folded down the center and closed, with the outer surface sometimes used for the address. Ironically, these tablets survived because they were thrown away: The garbage dump into which they were tossed provided a damp, anaerobic environment conducive to the preservation of the fragile wood. The tablet above seems to be a military memorandum concerning the fighting habits of the local British tribes. For another tablet from Vindolanda, see **141**.

...Brittones: Britto, Brittonis, c., *inhabitant of Britain, a Briton.* The interpretation of the letters preceding this word is not certain, but based on what can be made out, scholars have suggested "the Britons are unprotected by armor."

nimium: adv., *too much*, or, as here, *very*.

equites: eques, equitis, m., *horseman, cavalryman.*

residunt: resido, -sidere, -sedi, *to settle down*; of cavalry, *to mount.*

Brittunculi: Brittunculus, -i, m., *wretched little Briton*, a word found only here.

iaculos: otherwise unattested masc. form of iaculum, -i, n., *javelin.*

mittant: mitto, mittere, misi, missum, *to send, throw.*

135. Return Me To My Master (*CIL* 15.7193)

TENE ME NE
FVGIA · ET · REVO
CA ME AD DOMNVM
EVVIVENTIVM · IN
ARA CALLISTI

Tene me ne fugia<m> et revoca me ad dom<i>nu<m>
meu<m> Viventium in ar<e>a Callisti.

A slave collar found in Rome, now in the British Museum. On slave collars in ancient Rome, see **50.** The place where this slave is to be returned, the so-called *Area Callisti* ("Callistus's Square") was located in what is now Trastevere, on the west bank of the Tiber River.

revoca: revoco, -are, -avi, -atum, *to bring back.*
Viventium: Viventius, -i, m., *Viventius,* a proper name.
ar<e>a: area, -ae, f., *courtyard, open space, square.*
Callisti: Callistus, -i, m., *Callistus.*

136. Sensible Youth (*CIL* 9.2128, 7)

IVENIS TETENDI VT HABEREM QVOD VTERER

Iu<v>enis tetendi ut haberem quod uterer.

From an epitaph found near Beneventum (Benevento, Italy).

iu<v>enis: translate "as a young man."
tetendi: tendo, tendere, tetendi, tentum, *to strive, exert oneself.*

137. Foresight (*CIL* 5.6811)

FECI · QVOD · VOLVI · VIVVS · MONIMENTVM VBI · OSSA · ET · CINERES · AETERNVM · REQVIESCERENT· MIHI

**Feci quod volui vivus mon*u*mentum
ubi ossa et cineres aeternum requiescerent mihi.**

A grave inscription from Cisalpine Gaul (northern Italy), now lost. The mention of both bones and ashes reminds us that cremation in ancient Rome was different from cremation today. Unlike modern facilities, which achieve temperatures of over 1400° F., an ancient Roman cremation, conducted by means of a wood fire, generally did not reduce the remains completely to ash, but yielded a heap of ash admixed with smallish pieces of bone. In this inscription, the deceased characterizes his monument as, first and foremost, a place to house these remains.

> **vivus**: vivus, -a, -um, *alive, living*. Translate: "while living."
> **aeternum**: adverbial accusative, "for eternity."

XVIII.   Result Clause and Substantive Clause of Result

138. Sacred Space (*CIL* 5.7475)

ITA · TIBI · CONTINGANT QVAE · VIS · VT · TV · HOC SACRVM · NON · VIOLES

Ita tibi contingant quae vis ut tu hoc sacrum non violes.

An inscription found at Industria (Monteu da Po, Italy).

> **contingant**: contingo, -tingere, -tigi, -tactum, *to happen*.
> **sacrum**: sacrum, -i, n., *holy spot, sanctuary*.
> **violes**: violo, -are, -avi, -atum, *to violate, desecrate*.

139. The Illustrious Scipio Hispanus (*CIL* 1².15, 5-8; 6.1293; Courtney 13)

**VIRTVTES GENERIS MIEIS MORIBVS ACCVM[VL]AVI
PROGENIEM{I} GENVI FACTA PATRIS PETIEI
MAIORVM OPTENVI LAVDEM VT SIBEI ME ESSE CREATVM
LAETENTVR STIRPEM NOBILITAVIT HONOR**

**Virtutes generis meis moribus accumulavi,
progeniem genui, facta patris petii, maiorum
obtinui laudem ut sibi me esse creatum laetentur;
stirpem nobilitavit honor.**

From the epitaph of Gnaeus Cornelius Scipio Hispanus, found in an underground burial complex located along the *Via Appia*, just outside the Servian Wall in Rome. The complex contained the tombs of dozens of members of the aristocratic Scipio family. Despite the worthy resume we find inscribed elsewhere on the stone (praetor, aedile, quaestor, tribune of the soldiers, and other official positions), Scipio Hispanus was by no means the most distinguished representative of his clan. Note the archaic spellings, characteristic of the Latin used in the 2nd century BC (compare **43**, from the same period.)

generis: genus, generis, n., *family, clan.*
moribus: mos, moris, m., *habit, way*; plur., *character.*
accumulavi: accumulo, -are, -avi, -atum, *pile up, increase.*
progeniem: progenies, -ei, f., *offspring, descendants.*
genui: gigno, gignere, genui, genitum, *to beget, bear, produce.*
petii: peto, -ere, -ivi and -ii, -itum, *to seek, ask for; aim for, emulate.*
maiorum: masc. gen. plur. of maior, maius (comparative of magnus, -a, -um): "of my ancestors."
obtenui: obtineo, -tinēre, -tinui, -tentum, *to obtain, keep, uphold.*
laetentur: laetor, -ari, laetus sum, *to rejoice, be glad.*
me esse creatum: i.e., **me creatum esse**, accusative and infinitive depending on **laetentur**. From creo, -are, -avi, -atum, *to create, produce.*
stirpem: stirps, stirpis, f., *stock, root, family.*
nobilitavit: nobilito, -are, -avi, -atum, *to make renowned, to ennoble.*
honor: honor, honoris, f., *honor, esteem; public office, career.*

140. Reversal of Nature (*CIL* 9.5038, 5-7)

**QVOD · PAR · PARENTI · FACERE
FVERAT · FILIAM · MORS IMMATV
RA · FECIT · VT · FACERET · MATER · FILIAE**

**Quod par parenti facere fuerat filiam, mors
immatura fecit ut faceret mater filiae.**

From an epitaph found at Adria in Italy. The unnaturalness of parents burying their children is a common theme in Latin epitaphs. See also **106**.

> **par**: par, paris, *fair, suitable, appropriate, right.* Predicate with **fuerat**.
> **filiam**: acc. subj. of the infin. **facere**, dependent on **par**.
> **immatura**: immaturus, -a, -um, *immature, untimely.*

141. Birthday Invitation (*Tab. Vind.* 2.291)

CL SEVERA LEPIDINAE [SVAE
SA]L[V]TEM
III IDVS SEPTEMBR[E]S SOROR AD DIEM
SOLLEMNEM NATALEM MEVM ROGO
LIBENTER FACIAS VT VENIAS
AD NOS IVCVNDIOREM MIHI

[DIEM] INTERVENTV TVO FACTVRA

Cl(audia) Severa Lepidinae suae salutem. III Idus Septembres, soror, ad diem sollemnem natalem meum rogo libenter facias ut venias ad nos, iucundiorem mihi diem interventu tuo factura...

The first part of a birthday invitation from Claudia Severa to Sulpicia Lepidina, written in ink on a thin piece of wood excavated at the Roman fort at Vindolanda (Chesterholm, England). On the Vindolanda tablets, see **134**. This letter, along with two others by Claudia Severa, constitutes the earliest known specimen of Latin written by the hand of a woman. Further down on the tablet, in a different hand—presumably of Severa herself—is written, "I shall expect you, sister. Farewell, sister, my dearest soul, as I hope to prosper, and hail."

> **Cl(audia) Severa**: *Claudia Severa,* nom. sing.
> **Lepidinae**: dat. sing. of Lepidina, -ae, f., *Lepidina.*
> **salutem**: salus, salutis, f., *health, safety, wellbeing; greetings.* Dir. obj. of an
>   unexpressed **dat**, "sends."
> **III Idus Septembres**: Three days before the Ides of September, or
>   September 11th.
> **ad**: the **ad** before **diem** must be translated "for."
> **natalem**: natalis, -e, *having to do with birth*; with **diem**, *birthday.*
> **libenter**: "warmly." Goes with **rogo**.
> **facias**: "that you make sure."
> **iucundiorem**: iucundus, -a, -um, *pleasant, enjoyable.*
> **interventu**: interventus, -us, f., *appearance, arrival.*
> **factura**: fut. act. partic. showing purpose: "to make."

XIX.   Cum Clause

142. One Road (*CIL* 5.2411, 3)

QVID · QVERERIS · FATIS MORTIS CARISSIME · CONIVNX
CVM · SIT · COMMVNIS · OMNIBVS · VNA VIA

Quid quereris fatis mortis, carissime coniunx,
cum sit communis omnibus una via?

From an epitaph found near Ferrara, Italy. For the idea of death as the common destination of all mortals, see **113** and **143**. The words above are addressed by the deceased to her spouse.

   quereris: queror, queri, questus sum, *to complain.*
   fatis: Here, probably abl. object of an understood **de**: "about the fates."
   communis: communis, commune, *common, shared, universal.*

143. The Same End Awaits Us All (*CIL* 1².2138, 4-9; 5.4111)

HEVS · TV · VIATOR · LAS
SE · QVI · ME · PRAETER
EIS
CVM · DIV · AMBVLA
REIS · TAMEN · HOC
VENIVNDVM · EST · TIBI

Heus tu viator lasse, qui me praeter*is***, cum diu ambula(ve)r***is***, tamen hōc**
venи*en***dum est tibi.**

From an epitaph inscribed on a stone found near Mantua, Italy. For the idea of death as the common destination of all mortals, see **113** and **142**.

   heus: interjection, *hey!, hello!*
   lasse: lassus, -a, -um, *weary, tired.*
   praeteris: praetereo, -ire, -ivi and -ii, -itum, *to go past, pass by.*
   hōc: adv., *to this place; here.*

144. Lucius Caesar (*CIL* 6.36908; Gordon 30)

L CAESARI AVG[V]STI F DIVI N
PRINCIPI IVVENTV[TI]S COS DESIG
CVM [E]SSET ANN N[A]T XIIII AVG
SENATVS

L(ucio) Caesari, Augusti f(ilio), divi n(epoti),
principi iuventutis, co(n)s(uli) desig(nato) cum esset
ann(os) nat(us) XIIII, aug(uri), senatus.

Large inscribed marble block, dating to 2 BC, found broken into several pieces in the Roman Forum. Lucius Caesar was Augustus's grandson, the child of his daughter Julia and Marcus Agrippa. He is called the "son of Augustus" and "grandson of divine (Julius)" because of his adoption by the emperor at birth. A likely potential successor to Augustus, Lucius died four years after this inscription was commissioned. For Augustus, see **100**; for Julius Caesar, see **68**.

divi: divus, -a, -um, *divine, deified*. Refers to Julius Caesar.

n(epoti): nepos, nepotis, m., *grandson*.

principi iuventutis: an official title, *Prince of the Youth*, granted to Lucius and his brother Gaius, to designate them as potential heirs to the throne.

desig(nato): designatus, -a, -um, *elected, designate* (but not yet in office).

nat(us): nascor, nasci, natus sum, *to be born*.

XIIII: 14. The Romans regularly represented the number 4 with four vertical lines ("IIII"), in addition to the more familiar representation "IV."

aug(uri): augur, auguris, c., *augur, soothsayer*.

145. Temple of Isis, Destroyed by Earthquake (*CIL* 10.846; Keppie, p. 95)

N · POPIDIVS · N · F · CELSINVS
AEDEM · ISIDIS · TERRAE · MOTV · CONLAPSAM
A FVNDAMENTO · P · S · RESTITVIT · HVNC · DECVRIONES · OBLIBERALITATEM
CVM · ESSET · ANNORVM · SEX{S} · ORDINI · SVO · GRATIS · ADLEGERVNT

N(umerius) Popidius N(umeri) f(ilius) Celsinus aedem
Isidis terrae motu conlapsam a fundamento p(ecuniā)
s(uā) restituit. Hunc decuriones ob liberalitem, cum
esset annorum sex, ordini suo gratis adlegerunt.

Inscription found at Pompeii, recomposed from 37 pieces, recording the reconstruction of the Temple of Isis, which had been destroyed by an earthquake in AD 62. Temples to non Graeco-Roman deities like the Egyptian Isis were not uncommon in the Roman Empire. The unlikely circumstance of a 6 year-old benefactor paying for the reconstruction "with his own money" can be explained by the fact that his father, Numerius Popidius Ampliatus, a freedman, was barred from serving as a *decurio* (one of ten members of the municipal council), but his son, born to a free man, was not. Thus, Ampliatus used his money, in effect, to buy the position in the name of his son. This wealthy freedman was the inspiration for the character of the same name in Robert Harris's 2003 novel *Pompeii*. For another member of the Popidii clan, see **115**.

N(umerius) Popidius Celsinus: *Numerius Popidius Celsinus.*
aedem: aedes, aedis, f., *building, temple, house.*
Isidis: Isis, Isidis, f., the Egyptian goddess *Isis.*
motu: motus, -us, m., *movement.*
conlapsam: conlabor, conlabi, conlapsus sum, *to collapse, fall down in ruin.*
fundamento: fundamentum, -i, n., *basis, foundation.*
decuriones: decurio, decurionis, m., *member of the municipal council.*
liberalitem: liberalitas, -tatis, f., *kindness, generosity; gift.*
ordini: ordo, ordinis, m., *class, order, group.*
gratis: "without payment," i.e., the usual enrollment fee was waived.
adlegerunt: adlego, -legere, -legi, -lectum, *to choose, elect.*

XX. Indirect Question

146. All that is Left (*CIL* 1².1732, 3; 9.1837)

SI QVAERIS QVAE SIM CINIS EN ET TOSTA FAVILLA

Si quaeris quae sim, cinis en et tosta favilla.

From an epitaph found at Beneventum (Benevento, Italy). The deceased, Helvia Prima, is to be understood speaking the line. What conception of the afterlife is implied by this sentiment? How can this notion by reconciled with the statement made in **69**, from the same gravestone?

> **en**: interjection, *look!, behold!* Translate first in its clause.
> **tosta**: torreo, torrēre, torrui, tostum, *to burn*.
> **favilla**: favilla, -ae, f., *ashes, embers*.

147. Eternal Joys (*CIL* 6.17106, 2-4)

DVM VIXI · DIDICI · QVAE · MORS · QVAE · VITA · HOMINIS · ESSET AETERNA · VNDE · ANIMAE · GAVDIA · PERCIPIO

Dum vixi, didici quae mors, quae vita hominis esset, aeterna unde animae gaudia percipio.

Inscription found in Rome beneath a statue of a sitting philosopher. What conception of the afterlife is implied by the sentiment expressed here?

> **dum**: "while." On this use of dum, see **74**.
> **unde**: adv., *whence, from where*. Translate first in its clause.
> **percipio**: percipio, -cipere, -cepi, -ceptum, *to grasp, comprehend*.

148. Read On (*CIL* 5.5719)

**HOC · QVI · SCIRE · CVPIS · IACEANT · QVAE · MEMBRA SEPVLCRO
DISCES · DVM · RELEGAS · HOS · MODO · VERSICVLOS**

**Hōc qui scire cupis iaceant quae membra sepulcro,
disces dum relegas hos modo versiculos.**

An epitaph found near Mediolanum (Milan, Italy), now lost. Ironically, the identification of the deceased, promised to those who read the "little verses" that follow, was impossible at least as early as the 17th century, when it was noted that the next four lines of text were missing.

> **iaceant**: iaceo, -ēre, iācui, *to lie, lie dead, repose.*
> **membra**: membrum, -i, n., *limb.*
> **sepulcro**: sepulcrum, -i., n., *grave, tomb.*
> **disces**: disco, discere, didici, *to learn, get to know, come to understand.*
> **dum...modo**: conj., *provided that* (with subjunctive).
> **relegas**: relego, -legere, -legi, -lectum, *to read again.*
> **versiculos**: versiculus, -i., m., *little verse, little line.*

149. Faith, not Fear (*CIL* 8.18742)

**IN DEO SPERABO NON T
IMEBO · QVID MICHI FA
CIAT HOMO**

In Deo sperabo; non timebo quid mi*h*i faciat homo.

Psalms 55.11, inscribed on a confessional window found in Algeria (5th-6th c. AD).

XXI.   Indirect Command and Substantive Clause of Purpose

150. More Sage Advice

DVRVM CACANTES MONVIT VT NITANT THALES

Durum cacantes monuit ut nitant Thales.

From a wall painting in the Baths of the Seven Sages at Ostia. In this irreverent representation of seven famous Greek statesmen and thinkers of the early 6th century, they are imagined dispensing a different sort of wisdom than they were generally known for. See also 131.

> **nitant**: nitor, niti, nixus (or nisus), *to strain, exert oneself.* Note that by the standards of Classical Latin, the form **nitant** here is incorrect on two counts. First, the verb is treated as regular and not deponent, and second, the tense violates the rule of sequence of tenses. What would the correct Classical form be?
>
> **Thales**: *Thales*, nom. sing. The great thinker from Miletus (in present day Turkey), traditionally considered the first Greek philosopher.

151. Tomb of an Auctioneer (*CIL* 1².1210, 1; 6.32311; Courtney 18)

ROGAT · VT · RESISTAS · HOSPES T[E] HIC · TACITVS · LAPIS

Rogat ut resistas, hospes, te hic tacitus lapis.

From an epitaph inscribed on a marble tablet found in England. The deceased, Aulus Granius Stabilio, said to be the freedman of Marcus Granius, is described as a modest, frugal, and trustworthy man who, along with Marcus Granius, worked as an auctioneer (*praeco*). Note the oxymoron in *tacitus lapis...rogat.*

> **resistas**: resisto, -sistere, -stiti, *to stop, halt.*
> **tacitus**: tacitus, -a, -um, *silent, mute.*
> **lapis**: lapis, lapidis, m., *stone.*

152. Do Not Disturb (*CIL* 6.30104, 3)

ROGO NE SEPVLCRI VMBRAS VIOLARE AVDEAS

Rogo ne sepulcri umbras violare audeas.

From an epitaph found in Rome.

> **sepulcri**: sepulcrum, -i, n., *grave, tomb.*
> **umbras**: umbra, -ae, f., *shade, shadow, ghost.*

153. Getting Out the Vote (*CIL* 4.429; Wallace I.17)

**C · IVLIVM · POLYBIVM
AED · OVF · PANEM · BONVM ·FERT**

**Gaium Iulium Polybium aed(ilem) o(ro) v(os)
f(aciatis). Panem bonum fert.**

A dipinto from Pompeii, endorsing Gaius Julius Polybius for the position of aedile. Apparently Polybius's competence as a baker was considered a useful qualification for office. Numerous such election posters have been found painted on the walls of the city. For another example, see **42**.

Gaium Iulium Polybium: *Gaius Julius Polybius.*
aed(ilem): aedilis, aedilis, m., *aedile*, an elected position in Roman government responsible for, among other things, the administration of games.
f(aciatis): Classical Latin would say "ut faciatis."
panem: panis, panis, m., *bread.*

154. A Message to my Beloved (*CIL* IV.8364; Wallace II.141)

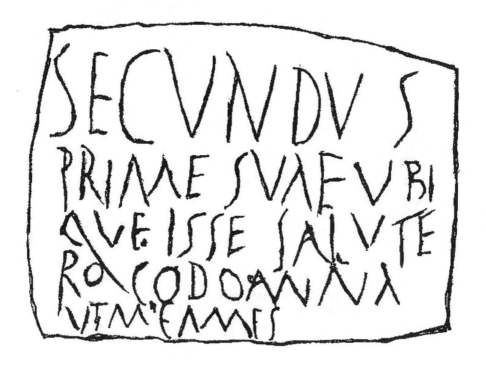

SECVNDVS
PRIME SVAE VBI
QVE ISSE SALVTE
ROGO DOMNA
VT ME AMES

Secundus Prim<a>e suae ubique ipse salute<m>:
rogo, dom<i>na, ut me ames.

A graffito from Pompeii. What are the literal meanings of the two names found
here? What does this suggest about Roman naming conventions?

Secundus: Secundus, -i, m., *Secundus*.
Prim<a>e: Prima, -ae, f., *Prima*.
ubique: *everywhere*.
salute<m>: salus, salutis, f., *health, safety, wellbeing; greetings*. What verb
is to be understood as governing this dir. obj.? (see **141**).
dom<i>na: domina, -ae, f., *lady, mistress; sweetheart*.

155. Titus Quinctius (Livy 6.29.9)

**Iuppiter atque divi omnes hoc dederunt, ut T(itus)
Quinctius dictator oppida novem caperet.**

An inscription mentioned by the Roman historian Livy (6.29.9). Titus Quinctius
Cincinnatus (not be confused with the more famous Lucius Quinctius
Cincinnatus), appointed dictator in 380 BC in response to a threat from the
inhabitants of Praeneste (modern Palestrina), led a successful attack which
brought it and eight neighboring towns under Rome's control. According to
Livy, Quinctius commemorated his achievement by dedicating on the Capitoline
Hill an image of Jupiter taken from Praeneste, accompanied by an inscription
"very much like" the text cited above (*his ferme incisa litteris*). Other sources
confirm that there was such a dedicatory plaque there, even if we cannot be
certain of its precise wording.

hoc: dir. obj. of **dederunt**, expanded by the **ut** clause that follows.
T(itus) Quinctius: *Titus Quinctius*.
dictator: dictator, dictatoris, m., *dictator*.
oppida: oppidum, -i, n., *town*.

156. Thirty-five Years of Marriage (*CIL* 6.16753)

D · M
DASVMIAE · SOTERIDI · LI
BERTAE · OPTIMAE · ET · CON
IVGI · SANCTISSIMAE · BENE
MER · FEC · L · DASVMIVS CAL
LISTVS · CVM · QVA · VIX · AN
XXXV · SINE VLLA · QVE
RELLA · OPTANS · VT · IPSA
SIBI · POTIVS · SVPERSTES · FV
ISSET · QVAM · SE · SIBI · SVPER
STITEM · RELIQVISSET

D(is) M(anibus). Dasumiae Soteridi libertae
optimae et coniugi sanctissimae bene mer(enti)
fec(it) Lucius Dasumius Callistus, cum quā vix(it)
an(nos) XXXV sine ullā querellā, optans ut ipsa sibi
potius superstes fuisset quam se sibi superstitem
reliquisset.

An epitaph found in Rome, now in the British Museum. One of many inscriptions that have been found commissioned by a husband for his wife.

Since marriages in ancient Rome were typically arranged by family members, they generally had more to do with practicality and compatibility than love (as the well-worn formula above, *sine ullā querellā*, seems to suggest). However, it is difficult not to see genuine affection in Lucius's regret that he must now live out the remainder of his life without his departed wife.

Dasumiae Soteridi: *Dasumia Soteris*, dat. sing.
libertae: liberta, -ae, f., *a freedwoman*.
Lucius Dasumius Callistus: *Lucius Dasumius Callistus*.
querellā: querella, -ae, f., *complaint*.
ipsa: subject of both **fuisset** and **reliquisset**.
potius...quam: "rather...than."
se sibi superstitem reliquisset: the first of these reflexives refers to
     Lucius, the second to Dasumia.
superstes: superstes, -stitis, *surviving, living beyond* (+ dat.).

XXII.   Conditions

157. The Power of Love (*CIL* 4.1649; Courtney 87; Wallace II.117)

ALLIGET · HIC · AVRAS · SI · QVIS
OBIVRGAT · AMANTES · ET · VETET
ASSIDVAS CVRRERE · FONTIS
AQVAS

**Alliget hic auras, si quis obiurgat amantes, et vetet
assiduas currere fontis aquas.**

A graffito from Pompeii. The thought is expressed as a condition, with *si quis obiurgat amantes* forming the prodosis, and *alliget hic auras* and *vetet assiduas currere fontis aquas* forming the two-part apodosis.

alliget: alligo, -are, -avi, -atum, *to tie up, bind*.
hic: subject of **alliget** and **vetet**, referring to **quis**.
quis: aliquis, aliquid, *someone, something, anyone, anything*.
obiurgat: obiurgo, -are, -avi, -atum, *to scold, disapprove of*.
assiduas: assiduus, -a, -um, *constant, unremitting*.
fontis: fons, fontis, m., *spring, fountain*.

158. Don't Even Think About It (*CIL* 4.1645; Courtney 93a; Wallace II.116)

SI · QVIS FORTE · MEAM · CVPIET · VIO[LARE]
PVELLAM · ILLVM · IN · DESERTIS
MONTIBVS · VRAT AMOR

Si quis forte meam cupiet violare puellam, illum in
desertis montibus urat amor.

A graffito from Pompeii, in the form of a condition with the jussive subjunctive *urat* in place of a future indicative in the apodosis. A similar graffito from the Palatine Hill, in addition to couching its protasis in much lewder terms, replaces *urat amor* with *ursus edat*: "may a bear eat him." For the metaphor of love as fire, see also **159**.

> **forte**: adv., *by any chance.*
> **desertis**: desertus, -a, -um, *deserted, wild.*
> **urat**: uro, urere, ussi, ustum, *to burn.*

159. Move It, Driver (*CIL* 4.5092, 1-2; Courtney 78; Wallace II.133)

AMORIS IGNES SI SENTIRES MVLIO
MAGI PROPERARES VT VIDERES VENEREM

Amoris ignes si sentires, mulio, magi<s> properares
ut videres Venerem.

A graffito from Pompeii, in which an desperate traveler urges his mule-driver to hurry up and take him to his beloved: *iamus, bibisti, iamus!* ("Let's go! You've had your drink, let's go!"). For the metaphor of love as fire, see **158**.

> **mulio**: mulio, mulionis, m., *mule-driver.*
> **magi<s>**: adv., *more.*
> **properares**: propero, -are, -avi, -atus, *to hurry, hasten.*
> **Venerem**: Venus, Veneris, f., the goddess *Venus*, or, by metonymy, *sexual love* or *a beloved.*

160. This Will Have to Do (*CIL* 6.15225, 3-6)

SI · PRO · VIRTVTE · ET · ANIMO
FORTVNAM · HABVISSEM · MAGNIFICVM · MONIMEN
TVM · HIC · AEDIFICASSEM · TIBI · NVNC · QVONIAM · OMNES
MORTVI · IDEM · SAPIMVS · SATIS · EST

Si pro virtute et animo fortunam habuissem,
magnificum monumentum hīc aedifica(vi)ssem tibi.
Nunc quoniam omnes mortui idem sapimus, satis est.

From an epitaph found in Rome. The words are addressed by a husband to his wife.

pro: "in accordance with."
aedifica(vi)ssem: aedifico, -are, -avi, -atus, *to build*.
mortui: mortuus, -a, -um, *dead, mortal*.
idem: idem, eadem, idem, *the same*. With **idem**, "have the same degree of perception."
sapimus: sapio, -ere, -ivi and -ii, *to sense, discern*.

161. Promise Cut Short (*CIL* 6.18324, 7-8)

QVOD · SI · LONGA · TVAE · MANSISSENT · TEMPORA · VITAE
DOCTIOR · IN TERRIS · NVLLA · PVELLA · FORET

Quod si longa tuae mansissent tempora vitae,
doctior in terris nulla puella foret.

From a tomb inscription found in Rome, marking the grave of a young girl named Dionysia.

quod: "but."
tempora: plural, but translate as singular.
doctior: doctus, -a, -um, *learned, accomplished*.
in terris: "on earth."
foret: 3rd pers. sing. imperf. subjunctive of sum, *to be*. A variant form of *esset*.

PART 5

Additional Inscriptions for Practice and Review

162. First Prize for Poetry (*CIL* 9.2860, 1-16)

L · VALERIO · L · F
PVDENTI
HIC · CVM · ESSET · ANNO
RVM · XIII · ROMAE
CERTAMINE · SACRO
IOVIS · CAPITOLINI
LVSTRO · SEXTO · CLA
RITATE · INGENII
CORONATVS · EST
INTER · POETAS · LA
TINOS · OMNIBVS
SENTENTIS · IVDICVM
HVIC · PLEBS · VNIVER
SA · MVNICIPVM · HIS
TONIESIVM · STATVAM
AERE · COLLATO · DECREVIT

L(ucio) Valerio L(ucii) f(ilio) Pudenti. Hic cum esset annorum XIII Romae certamine sacro Iovis Capitolini lustro sexto claritate ingenii coronatus est inter poetas Latinos omnibus sententi<i>s iudicum. Huic plebs universa municipum Histonie<n>sium statuam aere collato decrevit.

Inscription found at Histonium (Vasto, Italy), recording the prize awarded to a boy named Lucius Valerius Pudens for his poetry recitation at the the games held in honor of Jupiter Capitolinus in Rome. This competition can be dated to 106 AD, on the basis of the words "lustro sexto" in line 7. The final two lines of the inscription (not cited here) record that Pudens was later named to an official post by the emperor Antoninus Pius.

163. The Column of Trajan (*CIL* 6.960; Gordon 57))

SENATVS POPVLVSQVE ROMANVS
IMP CAESARI DIVI NERVAE F NERVAE
TRAIANO AVG GERM DACICO PONTIF
MAXIMO TRIB POT XVII IMP VI COS VI PP
AD DECLARANDVM QVANTAE ALTITVDINIS
MONS ET LOCVS TANTI[S OPE]RIBVS SIT EGESTVS

Senatus populusque Romanus imp(eratori) Caesari
divi Nervae f(ilio) Nervae Traiano Aug(usto)
Germ(anico) Dacico, pontif(ici) maximo,
trib(unicia) pot(estate) XVII, imp(eratori) VI, co(n)
s(uli) VI, p(atri) p(atriae), ad declarandum quantae
altitudinis mons et locus tantis operibus sit egestus.

Inscription on the base of Trajan's Column in Rome, considered to be among
the finest examples of Roman lettering to have come down to us. The column,
immensely important because of what its continuous spiral relief tells us about
the Roman army, was meant to provide a resting place for Trajan's ashes, as well
as a visual representation of the height of the hill that the emperor had removed
to clear a space for the construction of his extensive forum. On the column,
Trajan's official name reads "Caesar Nerva Traianus Augustus," to which the
titles "Germanicus" and "Dacicus" were added to commemorate his victories
in Germany and Dacia—the latter campaign being the one represented on the
spiral relief. The letters missing from the middle of the last line were destroyed
when the base of the column was used as a support for the roof of a medieval
church.

164. The Happiest Man in the World (CIL.14.636)

D M
P · AVFIDI · EPIC
TETI ·
VIXIT · ANNIS ·
LXXVII · MESI
· V · DIEBVS · XV ·
D · AVFIDI · M
HIC · IAM · NVNC · SITVS ·
EST · QVONDAM · PRAE
STANTIVS · ILLE · OMNIB
IN TERRIS · FAMA · VITAQVE
PROBATVS · HIC · FVIT · AD
SVPEROS · FELIX · QVO · NON ·
FELICIOR · ALTER · AVT FVIT
AVT ·VIXIT · SIMPLEX · BONVS ·
ATQVE · BEATVS · NVMQVAM
TRISTIS · ERAT · LAETVS ·
GAVDEBAT · VBIQVE · NEC SENIB
SIMILIS · MORTEM · CVPIEBAT
OBIRE · SET · TIMVIT · MORTEM
NEC · SE MORI · POSSE · PVTABAT
HVNC · CONIVNX · POSVIT · TERRAE
ET · SVA · TRISTIA · FLEVIT · VOL
NERA · QVAE · SIC · SIT · CARO · BIDV
ATA · MARITO

D(is) M(anibus) P(ublii) Aufidi Epicteti. Vixit annis LXXVII, me(n)si(bus) V, diebus XV. D(is) M(anibus) Aufidi. Hic iam nunc situs est quondam praestantius ille omnib(us) in terris fama vitaque probatus. Hic fuit ad superos felix, quo non felicior alter aut fuit, aut vixit. Simplex, bonus atque beatus, numquam tristis erat; laetus gaudebat ubique, nec senib(us) similis mortem cupiebat obire, sed timuit mortem nec se mori posse putabat. Hunc coniunx posuit terrae et sua tristia flevit vulnera, quae sic sit caro viduata marito.

Epitaph of Publius Aufidius Epictetus, found at Ostia, dating to the 2nd or 3rd c. AD. This is presumably the same man described in another inscription from Ostia as a grain merchant.

165. A Dog's Life (*CIL* 6.29896; Courtney 202)

GALLIA · ME · GENVIT · NOMEN · MIHI · DIVITIS · VNDAE
CONCHA · DEDIT · FORMAE · NOMINIS · APTVS · HONOS
DOCTA · PER · INCERTAS · AVDAX · DISCVRRERE · SILVAS
COLLIBVS · HIRSVTAS · ATQVE · AGITARE · FERAS
NON · GRAVIBVS · VINCLIS · VNQVAM · CONSVETA · TENERI
VERBERA · NEC · NIVEO · CORPORE · SAEVA · PATI
MOLLI · NAMQVE · SINV · DOMINI · DOMINAEQVE · IACEBAM
ET · NORAM · IN · STRATO · LASSA · CVBARE · TORO
ET · PLVS · QVAM · LICVIT · MVTO · CANIS · ORE · LOQVEBAR
NVLLI · LATRATVS · PERTIMVERE · MEOS
SED · IAM · FATA · SVBII · PARTV · IACTATA · SINSISTRO
QVAM · NVNC · SVB · PARVO · MARMORE · TERRA · TEGIT

MARGARITA

Gallia me genuit, nomen mihi divitis undae concha dedit, formae nominis aptus honos. Docta per incertas audax discurrere silvas collibus hirsutas atque agitare feras, non gravibus vinclis umquam consueta teneri verbera nec niveo corpore saeva pati. Molli namque sinu domini dominaeque iacebam et noram in strato lassa cubare toro, et plus quam licuit muto canis ore loquebar; nulli latratus pertimuerunt meos. Sed iam fata subii partu iactata sinistro, quam nunc sub parvo marmore terra tegit.

Margarita

Epitaph of a hunting dog named Margarita ("Pearl"), found in Rome, now in the British Museum. Hounds from Gaul were particularly prized in antiquity as hunting dogs and many of those, like Margarita, were also cherished as pets. While we often find dogs named in Roman epitaphs and sometimes even represented in sculpture, there are few that we know as well as Margarita, whose attributes and habits are described here in great detail.

166. Euhodus the Pearl Merchant (CIL 6.9545)

HOSPES RESISTE ET HOC AD GRVMVM AD LAEVAM ASPICE VBEI
CONTINENTVR OSSA HOMINIS BONI MISERICORDIS AMANTIS
PAVPERIS ROGO TE VIATOR MONVMENTO HVIC NIL MALE FECERIS
C ATEILIVS SERRANI L EVHODVS MARGARITARIVS DE SACRA
VIA IN HOC MONVMENTO CONDITVS EST VIATOR VALE
EX TESTAMENTO IN HOC MONVMENTO NEMINEM INFERRI NEQVE
CONDI LICET NISEI EOS LIB QVIBVS HOC TESTAMENTO DEDI TRIBVIQVE

Hospes, resiste et hoc ad grumum ad laevam aspice,
ub*i* continentur ossa hominis boni, misericordis,
amantis pauperis. Rogo, te, viator, monumento
huic nil male feceris. G(aius) Ateilius Serrani
l(ibertus) Euhodus, margaritarius de Sacra Via,
in hoc monumento conditus est. Viator, vale. Ex
testamento in hoc monumento neminem inferri
neque condi licet, nis*i* eos lib(ertos) quibus hoc
testamento dedi tribuique.

Epitaph found on the Appian Way outside of Rome, and still visible there today.

167. Flowers from Flavia (*CIL* 6.18385)

FLAVIA · NICOPOLIS · NOMEN · DVLCE · TVVM
ET · TVMVLO · SPARGAM · SAEPE · MEAS · LACRIMAS
O · MIHI · SI · SVPERI · VELLENT · PRAESTARE · ROGANTI
VT · TVO · DE · TVMVLO · FLOS · EGO · CERNA · NOVVM
CRESCERE · VEL · VIRIDI · RAMO · VEL · FLORE · AMARANTI
VEL · ROSEO · VEL · PVRPVREO · VIOLAEQVE · NITORE
VT · QVI · PRAETERIENS · GRESSV · TARDANTE · VIATOR
VIDERIT · HOS · FLORES · TITVLVM · LEGAT · ET · SIBI · DICAT
HOC · FLOS · EST · CORPVS · FLAVIAE · NICOPOLIS

Flavia Nicopolis. Nomen dulce tuum et tumulo spargam saepe meas lacrimas. O mihi si superi vellent praestare roganti ut tuo de tumulo flos ego cerna<m> novum crescere vel viridi ramo vel flore amaranti vel roseo vel purpureo violaeque nitore ut qui praeteriens gressu tardante viator viderit hos flores titulum legat et sibi dicat "hoc flos est corpus Flaviae Nicopolis."

From an epitaph found in Rome, dedicated by Titus Aelius Stephanus, a freedman of Augustus, to his departed wife, Flavia Nicopolis.

168. Imperial Messenger, Killed by Robbers (*CIL* 13.3689, 2-10)

QVI DOLET INTERITVM MENTEM SOLETVR AMORE
TOLLERE MORS VITAM POTVIT POST FATA SVPERSTES
FAMA VIGET PERIIT CORPVS SED NOMEN IN ORE EST
VIVIT LAVDATVR LEGITVR CELEBRATVR AMATVR
NVNTIVS AVGVSTI VELOX PEDE CVRSOR [VT AVRA]
CVI LATIAE GENTIS NOMEN PATRIAEQVE SABINVS
O CRVDELE NEFAS TVLIT HIC SINE CRIMINE MORTEM
DAMNATVS PERIIT DECEPTVS FRAVDE LATRONVM
NIL SCELVS EGISTI FAMA EST QVAE NESCIT OBIRE

Qui dolet interitum, mentem soletur amore. Tollere mors vitam potuit, post fata superstes fama viget. Periit corpus, sed nomen in ore est. Vivit, laudatur, legitur, celebratur, amatur nuntius Augusti, velox pede cursor ut aura, cui Latiae gentis nomen patriaeque Sabinus. O crudele nefas! tulit hic sine crimine mortem. Damnatus periit deceptus fraude latronum. Nil, scelus, egisti: fama est quae nescit obire.

Epitaph found at Augusta Treverorum (Trier, Germany), noteworthy for its many verbal echoes of Vergil's Aeneid. The deceased, Sabinus, was an agent of the cursus publicus, the postal system instituted by Augustus which had couriers and horses stationed at intervals along roads across the empire to carry messages efficiently over long distances. For these officials, as for most travelers in the ancient world, attack by bandits was a very real threat.

Suggestions for Further Reading

The Latin Language

Allen, W. Sydney. *Vox Latina. A Guide to the Pronunciation of Classical Latin*, 2nd ed. Cambridge, England, 1978.

Janson, Tore. *A Natural History of Latin*. Oxford, England, 1997.

Ostler, Nicholas. *Ad Infinitum: A Biography of Latin*. New York, 2007

Palmer, L.R. *The Latin Language*. London, 1954.

Inscriptions and Graffiti

Bowman, Alan K. *The Roman Writing Tablets from Vindolanda*. London, 1983.

Courtney, E. *Musa Lapidaria. A Selection of Latin Verse Inscriptions*. Atlanta, 1995.

Gordon, Arthur E. *Illustrated Introduction to Latin Epigraphy*. Berkeley, 1983.

Keppie, Lawrence. *Understanding Roman Inscriptions*. Baltimore, 1991.

LaFleur, Richard. *Scribblers, Scvlptors, and Scribes*. New York, 2010.

McCarthy, Brian C.J. *Latin Epigraphy for the Classroom*. Amherst, MA, 1992.

Sandys, J.E. *Latin Epigraphy: an Introduction to the Study of Latin Inscriptions*. Cambridge, England, 1919.

Shore, Paul. *Rest Lightly. An Anthology of Latin and Greek Tomb Inscriptions*. Wauconda, IL, 1997.

Wallace, Rex E. *An Introduction to Wall Inscriptions from Pompeii and Herculaneum*. Wauconda, IL, 2005.

General Reference

Adkins, Lesley and Roy A. Adkins. *Handbook to Life in Ancient Rome*. New York, 1994.

Carcopino, Jerome. *Daily Life in Ancient Rome: The People and the City at the Height of the Empire*. New Haven, 1968.

Cornell, Tim and John Mathews. *Atlas of the Roman World*. New York, 1982.

Crawford, Michael. *The Roman Republic*, 2nd ed. Cambridge, MA, 1992.

Shelton, Jo-Ann. *As the Romans Did: A Sourcebook in Roman Social History*, 2nd ed. Oxford, England, 1998.

Stambaugh, John E. *The Ancient Roman City*. Baltimore, 1988.

Wells, Colin. *The Roman Empire*, 2nd ed. Cambridge, MA, 1992.

Texts of Inscriptions without Notes and Vocabulary

1. Senatus populusque Romanus.

2. Labyrinthus. Hīc habitat Minotaurus.

3. Virum exspecto meum.

4. a. Marcus Spe<n>dusa<m> amat.

   b. Marcellum Fortunata cupit.

   c. Serena Isidoru<m> fastidit.

5. Restitutus multas decepit saepe puellas.

6. Rotas operā tenet Arepo sator.

7. Cinis sum, cinis terra est, terra dea est, ergo ego mortua non sum.

8. Hīc iacet Helpidius, fatis exstinctus iniquis, egregius iuvenis, causarum orator honestus.

9. Bonam vitam! Amo te. Ama me. Serva fidem.

10. Mercurius hīc lucrum promit<t>it, Apollo salutem, Septumanus hospitium cum prandio.

11. Fullones ululamque cano, non arma virumq(ue).

12. Terra tenet corpus, nomen lapis atque animam aer.

13. Balnea, vina, Venus corrumpunt corpora nostra, sed vitam faciunt b(alnea) v(ina) V(enus).

14. Nymfi<u>s subitaneā morte necatus, vixit breve tempus an(nos) V, m(enses) VI, d(ies) VIII.

15. O fatum infelicem, qui te nobis abstulit.

16. Senatus populusque Romanus divo Tito divi Vespasiani f(ilio) Vespasiano Augusto.

17. Deae Minervae et Herculi Victori.

18. Iam datus est finis vitae, iam pausa malorum.

19. A(uli) Suetti Certi aedilis familia gladiatoria pugnabit Pompeis pr(idie) K(alendas) Iunias. Venatio et vela erunt. A(uli) Suetti Certi aedilis familia gladiatoria pugnab(it) Pompeis pr(idie) K(alendas) Iunias. Venatio et vela erunt.

20. Puel<l>arum decus Celadus.

21. Otiosis locus hic non est. Discede, morator.

22. Iovi Optimo Maximo, deorum principi, gubernatori omnium rerum, caeli terrarumque rectori.

23. Vox ei grata fuit, pulsabat pollice c<h>ordas.

24. Quid mihi tam subito Maximus eripitur?

25.   Bono rei publicae nat(us).

26.   Solacio matri tu quoque Mater eras.

27.   Labora, aselle, quomodo ego laboravi, et proderit tibi.

28.   Tu, dea, tu pr<a>ese<ns>, nostro succurre labori.

29.   Tu nostri memento; nos numquam obliviscemur tui.

30.   Nil mali est, ubi nil est.

31.   Lucilla ex corpore lucrum faciebat.

32.   a. Staphilus hīc cum Quietā.

       b. Romula hīc cum Staphylo moratur.

33.   Campani, victoriā una cum Nucerinis periistis.

34.   Senatus populusque Romanus incendio consumptum restituit.

35.   Eximiā specie iacet hīc Priscilla puella.

36.   Telyphus, Samnis, natione T<h>rax.

37.   Amabili secutori. Nat(ione) Dacus, pug(navit) XIII, fato deceptus, non ab homine.

38.   Docta lyrā, grata et gestu, formosa puella hīc iacet aeternā Sabis humata domo.

39.   Uno minus quam bis denos ego vixi per annos integer, innocuus, semper piā
       mente probatus, qui docili lusu iuvenum bene doctus harenis pulcher et ille fui
       variis circumdatus armis.

40.   Vita brevis longo melior mortalibus aevo, nam parvo spatio floruit haec anima
       bis denos perfuncta annos sine crimine morum.

41.   Morborum vitia et vitae mala maxima fugi. Nunc careo poenis, pace fruor placidā.

42.   Lucretius hic Fronto dignus honore bono est.

43.   Hospes, quod dico paulum est, asta ac perlege. Hīc est sepulcrum hau<d>
       pulc<h>rum pulc<h>rae feminae. Nomen parentes nomina(ve)runt Claudiam.
       Suum maritum corde dilexit suo. Natos duos creavit; horum alterum in terrā
       linquit, alium sub terrā locat. Sermone lepido, tum autem incessu commodo.
       Domum servavit, lanam fecit. dixi. Abi.

44.   Cave canem!

45.   Bene lava!

46.   Salve, lucru<m>!

47.   Moram si quaeres, sparge miliu<m> et collige.

48.   Lalla, lalla, lalla, aut dormi aut lacte.

49.   Discite: Dum vivo, Mors inimica, venis.

50.   N(on) f(ui), f(ui), n(on) s(um), n(on) c(uro).

51.   Dum vixi, lusi.

52.   Vibius Restitutus hīc solus dormivit et Urbanam suam desiderabat.

53. Studia amavi, obsequens magistris fui, observavi parentorum praecepta, meos amicos colui.

54. Miximus in lecto; fateor, peccavimus, hospes. Si dices "quare?," nulla metella fuit.

55. Fugi. Tene me. Cum revoc*a*veris me d(omino) m(eo) Zonino, accipis solidum.

56. Gaudia, qu<a>e dederat, rapuit Fortuna repente.

57. Anima<m> mea<m> rapuerunt fata iniqua.

58. Dis Manibus. M(arco) Antonio Nigro, veterano Thraeci, qui vix(it) ann(os) XXXVIII, pugnavit XVIII. Flavia Diogenis coniugi suo bene merenti de suo fecit.

59. Factionis Venetae Fusco sacravimus aram de nostro, certi studiosi et bene amantes, ut scirent cuncti mon*u*mentum et pignus amoris. Integra fama tibi, laudem cursus meruisti, certa(vi)sti multis, nullum pauper timuisti, invidiam passus semper fortis tacuisti, pulchre vixisti, fato mortalis obi*i*sti.

60. Cornelia Helena amatur ab Rufo.

61. Hospitium hīc locatur. Triclinium cum tribus lectis.

62. Iam trahor in tenebras ducorq(ue) amplectere fratr(em).

63. Centauro vehitur rapta Deianira marito.

64. Seriolā parvā tam magna teneris.

65. Sic Fortuna tibi dederat transcurrere vitam, omnes mortales eādem nam sorte tenemur.

66. Bis hīc septeni mecum natales dies tenebris tenentur Ditis aeternā domu.

67. Apollonia quae vocitabar, lapide hōc inclusa quiesco.

68. Divo Iulio iussu populi Romani statutum est lege Rufrena.

69. Nunc data sum Diti, longum mansura per ae<v>um.

70. Zoticus hīc nomen nudum vanumq(ue) reliquit. In cineres corpus et in aethera vita soluta est.

71. Sex(tus) Aemilius Sex(ti) l(ibertus) Baro, frumentar(ius), in ignem inlatus est prid(ie) Non(as) Quinct(iles), Gn(aeo) Pompeio co(n)s(ule) tert(ium).

72. In hac cupā mater et filius positi sunt.

73. Helpidiae, bene merenti, quae vixit plus minus annis IX.

74. Dum vixi, bibi libenter. Bibite vos qui vivitis.

75. Vivite felices, superi, quorum fortuna beata (e)st.

76. Vivite felices, quibus est data vita fruenda.

77. Quod tu es, ego fui; quod nunc sum, et tu eris.

78. D(is) M(anibus). T(itus) Flavius Martialis hic situs est. "Quod edi, bibi, mecum habeo; quod reliqui, perdidi." V(ixit) a(nnos) LXXX.

79.   Hanc tibi quam vovi, posui, bone Iuppiter, aram praef(ectus) coh(ortis) nomine Gallonius.

80.   His requiesco locis, vitam cui fata nega(ve)runt.

81.   Procope manus *levo* contra Deum qui me innocentem sustulit, quae v<i>xit ann(os) XX. Pos(uit) Proclus.

82.   Hīc Perusina sita est, quā non pretiosior ulla femina.

83.   Ummidiae manes tumulus tegit iste, simulque Primigeni vernae, quos tulit una dies.

84.   Ars cui summa fuit fabricae, studium, doctrin(a) pudorque, quem magni artifices semper dix*erunt* magistrum. Doctior hōc nemo fuit, potuit quem vincere nemo, organa qui no(vi)sset facere aquarum aut ducere cursum.

85.   Qui legis hunc titulum, mortalem te esse memento.

86.   Pauper fuit aequo animo. Sci<e>bat mori*endum* sibi.

87.   Vivere me certe libuit dum vive*res* ipsa, sed modo morte tuā mors mihi sola placet.

88.   Admiror te, paries, non cecidisse qui tot scriptorum taedia sustineas.

89.   L(ucius) Licinius M(arci) f(ilius) Pol(lia) Nepos, cuius de vita merito pote<st> nemo queri, qui negotiando locupletem se speravit esse futurum, spe deceptus erat.

90.   Reliquisti mammam tuam gementem, plangentem, plorantem.

91.   Amans amanti haec tibi pro meritis do Caratus.

92.   Fumantes iterum cineres quid respicis, hospes?

93.   Tu qui carpis iter gressu properante, viator, siste gradu<m>, quaeso. Quod peto, parva mora est: oro ut praeteriens dicas, "s(it) t(erra) t(ibi) l(evis)."

94.   Deo Mithrae et soli invicto ab oriente ad occidentem.

95.   Locum religiosum per insolentiam erutum, virtut(i) et n(umini) Aug(usti) repurgatum, reddidit G(aius) Severius emeritus c(enturio) reg(ionis).

96.   Presbyter hīc situs est Celerinus nomine dictus, corporeos rumpens nexus qui gaudet in astris.

97.   Surr(e)c(turus) die caelo cum venerit auctor

98.   Lacrimas titulo noli, moriture, negare.

99.   Corpore consumpto, vivā animā, deus sum.

100. Senatus populusque Romanus imp(eratori) Caesari, divi Iuli f(ilio), co(n)s(uli) quinct(um), co(n)s(uli) design(ato) sext(um), imp(eratori) sept(imum), republicā conservatā.

101. Ursus togatus vitreā qui primus pilā lusi decenter cum meis lusoribus laudante populo maximis clamoribus thermis Traiani, thermis Agrippae et Titi, multum et Neronis, si tamen mihi creditis, ego sum.

102.   L(ucius) Mummi(us) L(uci) f(ilius) co(n)s(ul). Duct(u), auspicio imperioque eius
        Achaea capt(a est). Corint<h>o deleto Romam rediit triumphans. Ob hasce res
        bene gestas, quod in bello voverat, hanc aedem et signu(m) Herculis Victoris,
        imperator dedicat.

103.   Gn(aeus) Pompeius Magnus imperator, bello XXX annorum confecto, fusis
        fugatis occisis in deditionem acceptis hominum centiens viciens semel LXXXIII,
        depressis aut captis navibus DCCCXLVI, oppidis castellis MDXXXVIII in fidem
        receptis, terris a Maeotis ad Rubrum Mare subactis, votum merito Minervae.

104.   Ulterius nihil est morte neque utilius.

105.   Hōc iacet in tumulo secura Glyconis honesto. Dulcis nomine erat, animā quoque
        dulcior usque.

106.   Quod si longa magis duxissent fila sorores, aequius iste lapis complecteret ossa
        paterna.

107.   Dis Man(ibus). Comicus et Auriola, parentes infelicissimi, P(ublio) Licinio
        Successo. V(ixit) a(nnos) XIII, m(enses) I, d(ies) XIX.

108.   D(is) M(anibus). M(arcus) Ulpius Cerdo titulum posuit Claudiae Tycheni,
        coniugi carissim(ae), cum quā vix(it) annis II, mensibus VI, dieb(us) III, hor(is)
        X. In die mortis gratias maximas egi<t> apud deos et apud homines.

109.   Maximus hīc recubo dulcissimus infa<n>s bimulus in tertium escendens. Sis
        mihi, terra, levis. Dulcis eram matri, carior usque patri.

110.   Minimum malum fit contemnendo maximum.

111.   Nulla spes vivendi mihi sine coniuge tali: Illa domum servare meam, illa et
        consilio iuvare.

112.   Lugemus te, miserande puer, quia breve omne quod bonum est.

113.   Una domus cunctis nec fugienda viris.

114.   L(ucius) Fabricius G(ai) f(ilius) cur(ator) viar(um) faciendum curavit.

115.   V(ibius) Popidius Ep(idii) f(ilius) q(uaestor) porticus faciendas curavit.

116.   Admiranda loquor, quis autem credere possit?

117.   Noli dolere, mamma, faciendum fuit.

118.   Ne quis hīc urina<m> faciat.

119.   <Quis>quis amat, valeat; pereat, qui nescit amare; bis tanto pereat quisquis
        amare vetat.

120.   Duodecim deos et Dianam et Iovem Optimum Maximu<m> habeat iratos,
        quisquis hīc mixerit aut caca(ve)rit.

121.   Stercus intra cippos qui fecerit aut violarit, ne luminibus fruatur.

122.   Ne at<t>i<n>gas. Non sum tua; M(arci) sum.

123.   Adeste amici, fruamur tempus bonum, epulemur laeti, vita dum parva manet,
        Baccho madentes; hilaris sit concordia.

124.   Si sunt manes, sit tibi terra levis.

125.   Dic, rogo, praeteriens hospes, "Sit t(ibi) t(erra) levis et mol<l>iter ossa quiesc<a>nt."

126.   Felicem Aufidium Felicem semper deus faciat.

127.   Tu qui perleges, vivas, valeas, ames, ameris.

128.   Di vos bene faciant, amici, et vos, viatores, habeatis deos propitios.

129.   O utinam iunctos licuisset amore frui.

130.   Utinam nos fatus texisset utrosque.

131.   Ut bene caceret, ventrem palpavit Solon.

132.   Hi sancte coluerunt deos vixeruntque beati, post obitum Elysios ut possent visere
       campos.

133.   Paulo siste gradum, iuvenis pie, quaeso, viator, ut mea per titulum no(ve)ris sic
       invida fata.

134.   ...Brittones. Nimium multi equites. Gladi<i>s non utuntur equites nec residunt
       Brittunculi ut iaculos mittant.

135.   Tene me ne fugia<m> et revoca me ad dom<i>nu<m> meu<m> Viventium in
       ar<e>a Callisti.

136.   Iu<v>enis tetendi ut haberem quod uterer.

137.   Feci quod volui vivus monumentum ubi ossa et cineres aeternum requiescerent mihi.

138.   Ita tibi contingant quae vis ut tu hoc sacrum non violes.

139.   Virtutes generis meis moribus accumulavi, progeniem genui, facta patris petii,
       maiorum obtinui laudem ut sibi me esse creatum laetentur; stirpem nobilitavit honor.

140.   Quod par parenti facere fuerat filiam, mors immatura fecit ut faceret mater filiae.

141.   Cl(audia) Severa Lepidinae suae salutem. III Idus Septembres, soror, ad diem
       sollemnem natalem meum rogo libenter facias ut venias ad nos, iucundiorem
       mihi diem interventu tuo factura...

142.   Quid quereris fatis mortis, carissime coniunx, cum sit communis omnibus una via?

143.   Heus tu viator lasse, qui me praeteris, cum diu ambula(ve)ris, tamen hōc
       veniendum est tibi.

144.   L(ucio) Caesari, Augusti f(ilio), divi n(epoti), principi iuventutis, co(n)s(uli)
       desig(nato) cum esset ann(os) nat(us) XIIII, aug(uri), senatus.

145.   Isidis terrae motu conlapsam a fundamento p(ecuniā) s(uā) restituit. Hunc
       decuriones ob liberalitem, cum esset annorum sex, ordini suo gratis adlegerunt.

146.   Si quaeris quae sim, cinis en et tosta favilla.

147.   Dum vixi, didici quae mors, quae vita hominis esset, aeterna unde animae
       gaudia percipio.

148.   Hōc qui scire cupis iaceant quae membra sepulcro, disces dum relegas hos modo
       versiculos.

149. In Deo sperabo; non timebo quid mihi faciat homo.

150. Durum cacantes monuit ut nitant Thales.

151. Rogat ut resistas, hospes, te hic tacitus lapis.

152. Rogo ne sepulcri umbras violare audeas.

153. Gaium Iulium Polybium aed(ilem) o(ro) v(os) f(aciatis). Panem bonum fert.

154. Secundus Prim<a>e suae ubique ipse salute<m>: rogo, dom<i>na, ut me ames.

155. Iuppiter atque divi omnes hoc dederunt, ut T(itus) Quinctius dictator oppida novem caperet.

156. D(is) M(anibus). Dasumiae Soteridi libertae optimae et coniugi sanctissimae bene mer(enti) fec(it) Lucius Dasumius Callistus, cum quā vix(it) an(nos) XXXV sine ullā querellā, optans ut ipsa sibi potius superstes fuisset quam se sibi superstitem reliquisset.

157. Alliget hic auras, si quis obiurgat amantes, et vetet assiduas currere fontis aquas.

158. Si quis forte meam cupiet violare puellam, illum in desertis montibus urat amor.

159. Amoris ignes si sentires, mulio, magi<s> properares ut videres Venerem.

160. Si pro virtute et animo fortunam habuissem, magnificum monumentum hīc aedifica(vi)ssem tibi. Nunc quoniam omnes mortui idem sapimus, satis est.

161. Quod si longa tuae mansissent tempora vitae, doctior in terris nulla puella foret.

162. L(ucio) Valerio L(ucii) f(ilio) Pudenti. Hic cum esset annorum XIII Romae certamine sacro Iovis Capitolini lustro sexto claritate ingenii coronatus est inter poetas Latinos omnibus sententi(i)s iudicum. Huic plebs universa municipum Histonie(n)sium statuam aere collato decrevit.

163. Senatus populusque Romanus imp(eratori) Caesari divi Nervae f(ilio) Nervae Traiano Aug(usto) Germ(anico) Dacico, pontif(ici) maximo, trib(unicia) pot(estate) XVII, imp(eratori) VI, co(n) s(uli) VI, p(atri) p(atriae), ad declarandum quantae altitudinis mons et locus tantis operibus sit egestus.

164. D(is) M(anibus) P(ublii) Aufidi Epicteti. Vixit annis LXXVII, me(n)si(bus) V, diebus XV. D(is) M(anibus) Aufidi. Hic iam nunc situs est quondam praestantius ille omnib(us) in terris fama vitaque probatus. Hic fuit ad superos felix, quo non felicior alter aut fuit, aut vixit. Simplex, bonus atque beatus, numquam tristis erat; laetus gaudebat ubique, nec senib(us) similis mortem cupiebat obire, sed timuit mortem nec se mori posse putabat. Hunc coniunx posuit terrae et sua tristia flevit vulnera, quae sic sit caro viduata marito.

165. Gallia me genuit, nomen mihi divitis undae concha dedit, formae nominis aptus honos. Docta per incertas audax discurrere silvas collibus hirsutas atque agitare feras, non gravibus vinclis umquam consueta teneri verbera nec niveo corpore saeva pati. Molli namque sinu domini dominaeque iacebam et noram in strato lassa cubare toro, et plus quam licuit muto canis ore loquebar; nulli latratus pertimuerunt meos. Sed iam fata subii partu iactata sinistro, quam nunc sub parvo marmore terra tegit. Margarita.

166. Hospes, resiste et hoc ad grumum ad laevam aspice, ubi continentur ossa hominis boni, misericordis, amantis pauperis. Rogo, te, viator, monumento huic nil male feceris. G(aius) Ateilius Serrani l(ibertus) Euhodus, margaritarius de Sacra Via, in hoc monumento conditus est. Viator, vale. Ex testamento in hoc monumento neminem inferri neque condi licet, nisi eos lib(ertos) quibus hoc testamento dedi tribuique.

167. Flavia Nicopolis. Nomen dulce tuum et tumulo spargam saepe meas lacrimas. O mihi si superi vellent praestare roganti ut tuo de tumulo flos ego cerna<m> novum crescere vel viridi ramo vel flore amaranti vel roseo vel purpureo violaeque nitore ut qui praeteriens gressu tardante viator viderit hos flores titulum legat et sibi dicat "hoc flos est corpus Flaviae Nicopolis."

168. Qui dolet interitum, mentem soletur amore. Tollere mors vitam potuit, post fata superstes fama viget. Periit corpus, sed nomen in ore est. Vivit, laudatur, legitur, celebratur, amatur nuntius Augusti, velox pede cursor ut aura, cui Latiae gentis nomen patriaeque Sabinus. O crudele nefas! tulit hic sine crimine mortem. Damnatus periit deceptus fraude latronum. Nil, scelus, egisti: fama est quae nescit obire.

Vocabulary

A

a, ab, prep. + abl., *by, from*

abeo, -ire, -ii, -itum, *to go away, depart*

ac, conj., *and*

accipio, -cipere, -cepi, -ceptum, *to receive*

accumulo, -are, -avi, -atum, *to pile up, increase*

ad, prep. + acc., *to, toward*

adlego, -legere, -legi, -lectum, *to choose, elect*

admiror, -ari, admiratus sum, *to admire, be astonished at, wonder*

adsum, adesse, adfui, *to be present, be at hand*

aedes, aedis, f., *rooms, house; temple*

aedifico, -are, -avi, -atus, *to build*

aedilis, aedilis, m., *aedile*

aequus, -a, -um, *equal, even, level, fair, calm*

aes, aeris, n., *copper, bronze; money*

aer, aeris, m., *air, the air*

aeternus, -a, -um, *eternal*

aether, aetheris, m., *upper air, sky; heaven*

aevum, -i, n., *time, period of time, time of life, age*

agito, -are, -avi, -atum, *stir up; hunt, chase*

ago, agere, egi, actum, *to do, drive, conduct, act*

aliquis, aliquid, *someone, something; anyone, anything*

altitudo, -inis, f., *height, elevation*

alius, -a, -ud, *another, other; one...the other*

alligo, -are, -avi, -atum, *to tie up, bind*

alter, altera, alterum, *one of two; one...the other*

ambulo, -are, -avi, -atum, *to walk*

amicus, -i, m., *friend*

amo, -are, -avi, -atum, *to love*

amor, amoris, m., *love, passion, devotion*

amplector, -plecti, amplexus sum, *to embrace*

anima, -ae, f., *spirit, soul*

animus, -i, m., *mind, heart; courage, character*

annus, -i, m., *year*

Apollo, Apollinis, m., the god *Apollo*

aptus, -a, -um, *suitable, appropriate, fitting*

apud, prep. + acc., *at, among, at the house of*

aqua, -ae, f., *water*

ara, -ae, f., *altar, altar-tomb*

area, -ae, f., *courtyard, open space, square*

arma, -orum, n., *arms, weapons*

ars, artis, f., *art, craft; skill, expertise*

artifex, -ficis, m., *craftsman*

asellus, -i, m., *ass, donkey*

aspicio, -ere, -spexi, -spectum, *look at, behold*

assiduus, -a, -um, *constant, unremitting*

asto, astare, astiti, *to stop, stand still*

astrum, -i, n., *star, constellation*

atque, conj., *and, and also*

attingo, -ere, -tigi, -tactum, *to touch*
auctor, -oris, m., *originator, author; creator*
audax, audacis, *bold, daring*
audeo, -ēre, ausus sum, *to dare, venture*
aufero, auferre, abstuli, ablatum, *to carry off, steal*
augur, auguris, c., *augur, soothsayer*
aura, aurae, f., *breeze, wind*
auspicium, -i, n., *command, guidance, auspices*

B

balnea, balneorum, n., *baths, the baths*
beatus, -a, -um, *blessed, happy*
bellum, -i, n., *war*
bibo, bibere, bibi, bibitum, *to drink*
bimulus, -a, -um, *two years old*
bis, adv., *twice, two times*
bonus, -a, -um, *good*
brevis, -e, *brief, short*
Britto, Brittonis, c., *inhabitant of Britain, a Briton*
Brittunculus, -i, m., *wretched little Briton*

C

caco, -are, -avi, -atum, *to defecate*
cado, cadere, cecidi, *to fall, fall down; collapse*
caelum, -i, n., *sky, heaven*
campus, -i, m., *field, plain*
canis, canis, c., *dog*
cano, canere, cecini, cantum, *to sing, sing about*
capio, capere, cepi, captum, *to seize, capture*
Capitolinus, -a, -um, *Capitoline, of the Capitoline Hill*
careo, carēre, carui (+ abl.), *to lack, to be without*
carpo, carpere, carpsi, carptum, *to seize, pluck;* (with iter) *to proceed, make one's way*
carus, -a, -um, *dear, beloved*
castellum, -i, n., *fortress*
causa, -ae, f., *cause, reason; case, lawsuit*
caveo, -ēre, cavi, cautum, *to beware of, watch out for*
celebro, -are, -avi, -atum, *to celebrate, make known, honor*
Centaurus, -i, m., *a Centaur*
centurio, -onis, m., *a centurion*
certamen, -inis, n., *competition, contest*
certo, -are, -avi, -atum, *to contend with, compete against*
certus, -a, -um, *certain, steadfast, loyal*
chorda, -ae, f., *string* (of an instrument)
cinis, cineris, m., *ashes, ash*
cippus, -i, m., *stake, pillar, gravestone*
circumdo, -dare, -dedi, -datum, *to surround, gird, equip*
clamor, clamoris, m., *shouting*
claritas, -tatis, f., *brightness; shining distinction*
cohors, cohortis, f., *cohort, tenth part of a legion*
colligo, -ere, -legi, -lectum, *to gather, pick up*
collis, collis, m., *hill*
colo, colere, colui, cultum, *to inhabit, cultivate; honor, cherish, worship*

commodus, -a, -um, *agreeable, pleasing*
communis, commune, *common, shared, universal*
complector, -plecti, -plexus sum, *to embrace, encircle, surround*
concha, -ae, f., *oyster*
concordia, -ae, f., *friendship, fellowship*
condo, -ere, -didi, -ditum, *to found, establish; bury*
confero, -ferre, -tuli, -latum, *to gather, collect*
conficio, -ficere, -feci, -fectum, *to finish, complete*
coniunx, coniugis, c., *spouse*
conlabor, conlabi, conlapsus sum, *to collapse, fall down in ruin*
conservo, -are, -avi, -atum, *to keep, preserve*
consilium, -i, n., *counsel, advice*
consuetus, -a, -um, *accustomed*
consul, consulis, m., *consul*
consumo, -sumere, -sumpsi, -sumptum, *to consume, destroy*
contemno, -temnere, -tempsi, -temptum, *to despise, disdain, neglect*
contineo, -ēre, -tinui, -tentum, *to contain, enclose*
contingo, -tingere, -tigi, -tactum, *to happen*
contra, prep. + acc., *against*
cor, cordis, n., *heart*
corono, -are, -avi, -atum, *to crown, wreathe*
corporeus, -a, -um, *bodily, corporeal*
corpus, -oris, n., *body*
corrumpo, -rumpere, -rupi, -ruptum, *to weaken, destroy*
credo, credere, credidi, creditum (+ dat.), *to believe*
creo, -are, -avi, -atum, *to create, produce*
cresco, crescere, crevi, cretus, *to spring up, grow*
crimen, criminis, n., *charge, blame, crime*
crudelis, -e, *cruel, fierce, harsh*
cubo, -are, cubui, cubitum, *to lie down*
cum, conj., *when, since, although*
cum, prep. + abl., *with*
cunctus, -a, -um, *all*
cupa, -ae, f., *niche*
cupio, -ere, cupivi and cupii, cupitum, *to desire, wish*
curator, -oris, m., *overseer, superintendent*
curro, currere, cucurri, cursum, *to run; flow*
cursor, -oris, m., *courier, runner*
cursus, -us, m., *course; speed; channel*

D

Dacus, -a, -um, *Dacian*
damno, -are, -avi, -atum, *to condemn, sentence, doom*
de, prep. + abl., *from, down from; concerning, about*
dea, -ae, f., *goddess*
decenter, adv., *properly, pleasingly, gracefully*
decerno, -ere, -crevi, -cretum, *to decree*
decipio, -cipere, -cepi, -ceptum, *to catch, deceive, foil, cheat*
declaro, -are, -avi, -atum, *to declare, make clear, demonstrate*
decurio, decurionis, m., *member of the municipal council*
decus, decoris, n., *glory*
deditio, -ionis, f., *surrender*

deleo, -ēre, -evi, -etum, *to destroy*
deprimo, -primere, -pressi, -pressum, *to sink*
desertus, -a, -um, *deserted, wild*
desidero, -are, -avi, -atum, *to long for, miss*
designatus, -a, -um, *elected, designate*
deus, -a, -um, *divine, immortal*
deus, -i, m., *god*
Diana, -ae, f., the goddess *Diana*
dico, dicere, dixi, dictum, *to say, speak; name, call*
dictator, dictatoris, m., *dictator*
dies, diei, f., *day*
dignus, -a, -um, *worthy of* (+ abl.)
diligo, -ligere, -lexi, -lectum, *to love, cherish*
Dis Manibus, *to the departed spirits*
Dis, Ditis, m., *Dis,* ruler of the underworld
discedo, -cedere, -cessi, -cessum, *to leave, depart*
disco, discere, didici, *to learn, get to know, come to understand*
discurro, -currere, -cucurri, -cursum, *to run around, race*
dives, divitis, *rich, abundant*
divus, -a, -um, *divine; deified*
do, dare, dedi, datum, *to give*
docilis, -e, *teachable, skilful*
doctrina, -ae, f., *learning, training*
doctus, -a, -um, *learned, accomplished*
doleo, dolēre, dolui, *to suffer pain, grieve*
domina, -ae, f., *lady, mistress; sweetheart*
dominus, -i, m., *master*
domus, -us, f., *home*
dormio, -ire, -ivi, -itum, *to sleep*
duco, ducere, duxi, ductum, *to lead, to draw along, produce*
ductus, -us, m., *command, leadership*
dulcis, -e, *sweet*
dum, conj., *while, so long as, provided that*
duo, -ae, -o, *two*
duodecim, *twelve*

E

e/ex, prep. + abl., *out of, out from; in accordance with*
edo, edere, edi, esum, *to eat*
egero, -ere, egessi, egestum, *to remove, take away*
ego, *I*
egregius, -a, -um, *excellent, outstanding*
Elysius, -a, -um, *Elysian*
emeritus, -a, -um, *veteran, retired*
en, interj., *look!, behold!*
epulor, epulari, epulatus sum, *to feast*
eques, equitis, m., *horseman, cavalryman*
ergo, adv., *therefore*
eripio, -ripere, -ripui, -reptum, *to snatch away*
eruo, -ere, -ui, -utum, *to destroy, demolish*
escendo, -scendere, -scendi, -scensum, *to ascend, advance, approach*
eximius, -a, -um, *exceptional, distinguished*

exspecto, -are, -avi, -atum, *to wait for*
exstinguo, -stinguere, -stinxi, -stinctum, *to extinguish; to kill, destroy*

F

fabrica, -ae, f., *workmanship, craftsmanship*
facio, facere, feci, factum, *to make, do*
factio, factionis, f., *team, faction*
fama, -ae, f., *rumor, reputation, renown*
familia, -ae, f., *family, household; group*
fastidio, -ire, -ivi, -itum, *to despise*
fateor, fateri, fasus sum, *to confess, admit*
fatum, -i, n., *fate*
fatus, -i, m., *fate*
favilla, -ae, f., *ashes, embers*
felix, felicis, *happy, joyful, blessed; lucky, prosperous*
femina, -ae, f., *woman*
fera, -ae, f., *wild animal*
fero, ferre, tuli, latum, *to carry, carry off, bear; produce, make*
fides, fidei, f., *faith, trust, reliance, faithfulness*
filia, -ae, f., *daughter*
filius, -i, m., *son*
finis, finis, m., *end*
fio, fieri, factus sum, *to become, be made*
fleo, flēre, flevi, fletum, *to bewail, lament, weep over*
floreo, -ēre, -ui, *to bloom, flower, blossom, flourish*
flos, floris, m. or n., *flower, blossom*
fons, fontis, m., *spring, fountain*
forma, -ae, f., *appearance; beauty*
formosus, -a, -um, *beautiful*
forte, adv., *by any chance*
fortis, -e, *brave, strong, resolute*
fortuna, -ae, f., *chance, fate, luck, fortune; wealth, property*
frater, fratris, m., *brother*
fraus, fraudis, f., *trick, deception; injury*
frumentarius, -i, m., *grain merchant*
fruor, frui, fructus sum (+ abl.), *to enjoy*
fugio, fugere, fugi, fugitum, *to flee, escape*
fugo, -are, -avi, -atum, *to put to flight*
fullo, fullonis, m., *a launderer*
fumo, fumare, fumavi, *to smoke, steam*
fundamentum, -i, n., *basis, foundation*
fundo, fundere, fudi, fusum, *to rout, scatter*

G

Gallia, -ae, f., *Gaul*
gaudeo, gaudēre, gavisus sum, *to rejoice*
gaudium, -i, n., *joy, pleasure*
gemo, gemere, gemui, gemitum, *to sigh, lament*
gens, gentis, f., *race, tribe, people*
genus, generis, n., *family, clan*
gero, gerere, gessi, gestum, *to wage, do, accomplish, carry out*
gestus, -us, m., *posture; the gestures of a performer*

gigno, gignere, genui, genitum, *to bear, produce, give birth to*
gladiatorius, -a, -um, *gladiatorial*
gladius, -i, m., *sword*
gradus, -us, m., *step, pace*
gratia, -ae, f., *favor, kindness, thanks*
gravis, grave, *heavy, weighty; severe.*
gressus, -us, m., *step, course*
grumus, -i, m., *mound, little hill*
gubernator, -oris, m., *steerer, governor*

<h1 style="text-align:center">H</h1>

habeo, -ēre, -ui, -itum, *to have, hold, consider*
habito, -are, -avi, -atum, *to live, dwell*
harena, -ae, f., *sand; the arena in the amphitheatre*
haud, adv., *by no means, not at all*
Hercules, -is, m., *Hercules*
heus, interj., *hey!, hello!*
hīc, adv., *here*
hic, haec, hoc, *this*
hilaris, -e, *cheerful, merry*
hirsutus, -a, -um, *rough, shaggy, bristling*
Histoniensis, -e, *of or belonging to the town of Histonium*
hōc, adv., *to this place, here*
homo, hominis, m., *man, human being*
honestus, -a, -um, *honorable, respectable, distinguished*
honor, honoris, f., *honor, esteem; distinction public office, career*
honos, see *honor*
hora, -ae, f., *hour*
hospes, hospitis, m., *guest, host, stranger, passerby*
hospitium, -i, n., *hospitality; an inn, lodging*
humo, -are, -avi, -atum, *to bury*

<h1 style="text-align:center">I</h1>

iaceo, iacēre, iacui, *to lie, lie dead, repose*
iacto, -are, -avi, -atum, *to throw around; disturb, torment*
iaculum, -i, n., *javelin*
iam, adv., *now, already*
incertus, -a, -um, *uncertain, obscure*
idem, eadem, idem, *the same*
Idus, Iduum, f. the *Ides,* the thirteenth or fifteenth day of the Roman month
ignis, ignis, m., *fire*
ille, illa, illud, *that; he, she, it*
immaturus, -a, -um, *immature, untimely*
imperator, -oris, m., *commander, leader; emperor*
imperium, -i, n., *power, authority*
in, prep. + abl., *in, among*
in, prep. + acc., *into, against*
incendium, -i, n., *fire, conflagration*
incessus, -us, m., *bearing, gait*
includo, -ere, inclusi, inclusum, *to shut in, enclose*
infans, infantis, c., *infant, young child*
infelix, infelicis, *unlucky, woeful; unhappy, miserable*

infero, inferre, intuli, inlatum, *to bring in, place on*
ingenium, -ii, n., *genius, talent, ability*
inimicus, -a, -um, *unfriendly, hateful*
iniquus, -a, -um, *adverse, unfair, unfavorable*
innocens, -entis, *innocent, blameless*
insolentia, -ae, f., *insolence, arrogance*
inter, prep + acc, *among, amid, between*
integer, -gra, -grum, *uncorrupted, upright*
interitus, -us, m., *death*
interventus, -us, f., *appearance, arrival*
intra, prep. + acc., *within, inside*
invictus, -a, -um, *unconquered*
invidia, -ae, f., *envy, jealousy, ill-will*
invidus, -a, -um, *envious, hateful, unfavorable*
iratus, -a, -um, *angry*
is, ea, id, *he, she, it; this, that*
Isis, Isidis, f., the Egyptian goddess *Isis*
iste, ista, istud, *that*
ita, adv., *so, thus, in such a way*
iterum, adv., *again, a second time*
iucundus, -a, -um, *pleasant, enjoyable*
iudex, iudicis, m., *judge*
iungo, iungere, iunxi, iunctum, *to join, unite*
Iunius, -a, -um, *of June*
Iuppiter, Iovis, m., the god *Jupiter*
iuvenis, iuvenis, c., *young man, young woman; member of the* Iuvenes
iuvenis, iuvenis, *young*
iuventus, -tutis, f., *youth, young men*
iuvo, -are, iuvi, iutum, *to help*

K

Kalendae, -arum, f., *Kalends,* the first day of the Roman month

L

labor, -oris, m., *work, labor; distress, suffering*
laboro, -are, -avi, -atum, *to work*
labyrinthus, -i, m., *labyrinth*
lacrima, -ae, f., *tear*
lacteo, -ēre, *to suckle, nurse*
laetor, -ari, laetus sum, *to rejoice, be glad*
laetus, -a, -um, *happy, joyful*
laevus, -a, -um, *left, the left side*
lana, -ae, f., *wool*
lapis, lapidis, m., *stone*
lassus, -a, -um, *weary, tired*
Latinus, -a, -um, *Latin, having to do with the Latin language*
Latius, -a, -um, *of or belonging to Latium, Latin*
latratus, -us, m., *barking*
latro, -onis, m., *robber, bandit, highwayman*
laudo, -are, -avi, -atum, *to praise*
laus, laudis, f., *praise, fame, glory*
lavo, -are, -avi, -atum, *to wash, bathe*

lectus, -i, m., *couch, bed*
lego, legere, legi, lectum, *to read*
lepidus, -a, -um, *pleasant*
levis, levis, *light, not heavy*
levo, -are, -avi, -atum, *to raise, lift up*
lex, legis, f., *law*
liberalitas, -tatis, f., *kindness, generosity; gift*
liberta, -ae, f., *freedwoman*
libertus, -i, m., *freedman*
libet, libēre, libuit or **libitum est** (impersonal), *it pleases, it is agreeable*
licet, licēre, licuit (impersonal), *it is allowed*
linquo, linquere, liqui, *to leave, leave behind, abandon, forsake*
loco, -are, -avi, -atum, *to locate, place, put*
locuples, -pletis, *rich*
locus, -i, m., *place, location*
longus, -a, -um, *long*
loquor, loqui, locutus sum, *to say, speak*
lucrum, -i, n., *profit*
ludo, ludere, lusi, lusum, *to play*
lugeo, lugēre, luxi, *to mourn*
lumen, -inis, n., *light; eye*
lusor, -oris, m., *player*
lustrum, -i, n., *period of five years; religious cycle*
lusus, -us, m., *game, sport*
lyra, -ae, f., *the lyre; lyric poetry*

M

madeo, madēre, *to be wet, soaked; to be drunk*
magis, adv., *more*
magister, magistri, m., *teacher, master*
magnus, -a, -um, *large, great*
malus, -a, -um, *bad, evil*
mamma, -ae, f., *mama*
maneo, manēre, mansi, mansum, *to remain, stay, endure*
manes, -ium, m., *shades of the departed, spirits of the dead*
manus, us, f., *hand*
margarita, -ae, f., *pearl*
margaritarius, -i, m., *pearl merchant*
maritus, -i, m., *husband*
marmor, -oris, n., *marble; a block of marble*
mater, matris, f., *mother*
maximus, -a, -um, *greatest,* superlative of magnus
membrum, -i, n., *limb*
memini, meminisse (+ gen.), *to remember*
mens, mentis, f., *mind, judgement, disposition*
mensis, mensis, m., *month*
Mercurius, -i, m., *the god Mercury*
mereo, -ēre, -ui, -itum, *to deserve, be deserving, merit*
meritum, -i, n., *merit, desert*
metella, -ae, f., *chamber-pot*
meus, -a, -um, *my, mine*
milium, -i, n., *millet (a kind of grain)*

Minerva, -ae, f., the goddess *Minerva*
mingo, mingere, minxi and **mixi, mictum,** *to urinate*
Minotaurus, -i, m., *the Minotaur*
misericors, -cordis, *compassionate*
miseror, miserari, miseratus sum, *to pity*
Mithras, -ae, m., the Persian god *Mithras*
mitto, mittere, misi, missum, *to send, throw*
mollis, -e, *soft*
molliter, adv., *easily, gently*
mons, montis, m., *mountain*
monumentum, -i, n., *monument, memorial, record*
mora, -ae, f., *delay; a way to waste time*
morator, -oris, m., *delayer, loiterer*
morbus, -i, m., *sickness, disease*
morior, mori, mortuus sum, *to die*
moror, -ari, moratus sum, *to delay, linger, loiter, stay*
mors, mortis, f., *death*
mortalis, -e, *mortal, human*
mortuus, -a, -um, *dead*
mos, moris, m., *habit, way;* (plur.) *character*
motus, -us, m., *movement*
mulio, mulionis, m., *mule-driver*
multus, -a, -um, *much, many*
municeps, -cipis, c., *citizen, townsman*
mutus, -a, -um, *mute, speechless*

N

nam, conj., *for*
namque, *for; and in fact*
nascor, -i, natus, *to be born*
natalis, -e, *having to do with birth*
natio, nationis, m., *birth, nationality*
natus, -i, m., *son*
ne, adv. and conj., *not, lest, that not*
nec, conj., *nor, and not*
neco, -are, -avi, -atum, *to kill*
nefas (indeclinable), *impious deed, crime*
nego, -are, -avi, -atum, *to deny, refuse*
negotio, -are, -avi, -atum, *to conduct business*
nemo, neminis, c., *no one, nobody*
nepos, nepotis, m., *grandson*
nescio, -ire, -ivi and -ii, -itum, *to not know (how)*
nexus, -us, m., *a binding; restraint*
nihil, *nothing*
nil, see *nihil*
nimium, adv., *much, a great deal, very*
nisi, *if not, unless*
nitor, niti, nixus or nisus sum, *to strain, exert oneself*
nitor, -oris, m., *brightness, splendor, sheen*
niveus, -a, -um, *snowy, snow-white*
nobilito, -are, -avi, -atum, *to make renowned, to ennoble*
nolo, nolle, nolui, *to be unwilling, not want;* (imperat.) *don't*

nomen, nominis, n., *name*
nomino, -are, -avi, -atum, *to name, call*
non, adv., *not*
Nonae, -arum, f., *Nones,* the fifth or seventh day of the Roman month
nosco, noscere, novi, notum, *to become acquainted with;* (perf.) *to know*
noster, nostra, nostrum, *our*
novem, *nine*
novus, -a, -um, *fresh*
nudus, -a, -um, *naked, bare*
nullus, -a, -um, *no, none*
numen, -inis, n., *divinity, divine spirit, living spirit*
numquam, adv., *never*
nunc, adv., *now*
nuntius, -i, m., *messenger*

O

O, interjection, *o, oh*
ob, prep. + acc., *because of, on account of*
obeo, -ire, -ivi and **-ii, itum,** *to go to meet; to go to meet death, to die*
obitus, -us, m., *death*
obiurgo, -are, -avi, -atum, *to scold, disapprove of*
obliviscor, oblivisci, oblitus sum (+ gen.), *to forget*
obsequens, -ntis, *yielding, compliant, obedient*
observo, -are, -avi, -atum, *to pay attention to, heed*
obtineo, -tinēre, -tinui, -tentum, *to obtain, keep, uphold*
occido, -ere, -cidi, -casum, *to fall;* (of the sun) *to set*
occido, -ere, -cidi, -cisum, *to kill*
omnis, omne, *all, every*
opera, -ae, f., *effort, care*
oppidum, -i, n., *town*
optimus, -a, -um, *best,* superlative of bonus
opto, -are, -avi, -atum, *to wish*
opus, -eris, n., *work*
orator, -oris, m., *orator, speaker, pleader*
ordo, ordinis, m., *class, order, group*
organum, -i, n., *instrument, equipment*
orior, oriri, ortus sum, *to rise*
oro, -are, -avi, -atum, *to beg, pray, entreat*
os, oris, n., *mouth*
os, ossis, n., *bone*
otiosus, -a, -um, *idle, at leisure*

P

palpo, -are, -avi, -atum, *to stroke, pat*
panis, panis, m., *bread*
par, paris, *fair, suitable, appropriate, right*
parens, parentis, c., *parent*
paries, -ietis, m., *wall*
parvus, -a, -um, *small*
pater, patris, m., *father*
paternus, -a, -um, *paternal, relating to a father, a father's*
patior, pati, passus sum, *to suffer, endure, experience*

partus, -us, m., *birth, delivery*
parvus, -a, -um, *small*
patria, -ae, f., *fatherland, one's native country*
paulus, -a, -um, *little, small, short*
pauper, -eris, m., *a poor man*
pausa, pausae, f., *pause, end*
pax, pacis, f., *peace*
pecco, peccare, peccavi, peccatum, *to make a mistake, to do wrong*
pecunia, -ae, f., *money*
per, prep. + acc., *through, throughout; on account of*
percipio, -cipere, -cepi, -ceptum, *to grasp, comprehend*
perdo, -ere, -didi, -ditum, *to waste, lose; destroy*
pereo, -ire, -ivi and **-ii, itum,** *to perish, die*
perfungor, -fungi, -functus sum, *to go through, complete*
perlego, -legere, -legi, -lectum, *to read through, read carefully*
pertimesco, -ere, -timui, *to be afraid of*
pes, pedis, m., *foot*
peto, -ere, petivi, petitum, *to seek, ask for; aim for, emulate*
pignus, -oris, n., *pledge, token, proof*
pila, -ae, f., *ball*
pius, -a, -um, *dutiful, patriotic, godly, kind*
placeo, -ēre, -ui, -itum, *to please, be agreeable to*
placidus, -a, -um, *quiet, gentle, calm*
plango, plangere, planxi, planctum, *to wail, bewail*
plebs, plebis, f., *the people; population*
ploro, -are, -avi, -atum, *to cry aloud in grief, to weep over*
poena, -ae, f., *punishment, hardship, penalty, fine*
poeta, -ae, m., *poet*
pollex, -icis, m., *thumb*
Pompei, -orum, m., *Pompeii*
pono, ponere, posui, positum, *to put, place; set up, erect*
Pontifex Maximus, *Pontifex Maximus, the chief priest at Rome*
populus, -i, m., *people*
porticus, -us, f., *portico, colonnade*
possum, posse, potui, *to be able*
post, prep. + acc., *behind, after*
potestas, -tatis, f., *power, authority*
potius, adv., *rather, more, preferably*
praeceptum, -i, n., *lesson, teaching, command*
praefectus, -i, m., *commander, prefect*
praesens, -entis, *present; propitious*
praestans, praestantis, *outstanding, excellent*
praesto, -stare, -stiti, -stitum, *excel, surpass; vouch (for); take care (that)*
praetereo, -ire, -ivi and **-ii, -itum,** *to go past, pass by*
prandium, -i, n., *lunch, late breakfast*
presbyter, -teri, m., *priest*
pretiosus, -a, -um, *precious, dear*
pridie, adv., *on the day before*
primus, -a, -um, *first*
princeps, principis, m., *leader, chief, prince*
pro, prep. + abl., *before; for, on behalf of; in accordance with*
probo, -are, -avi, -atum, *to approve, endorse*

progenies, -ei, f., *offspring, descendants*
promitto, -mittere, -misi, -missum, *to promise*
propero, -are, -avi, -atum, *to hasten, hurry*
propitius, -a, -um, *propitious, favorable*
prosum, prodesse, profui (+ dat.), *to be useful, do good, benefit*
pudor, pudoris, m., *modesty, decency, honor*
puella, -ae, f., *girl*
pugno, -are, -avi, -atum, *to fight*
pulcher, -chra, -chrum, *beautiful, handsome; noble*
pulso, -are, -avi, -atum, *to beat, strike, pluck*
purpureus, -a, -um, *purple-colored*
puto, -are, -avi, -atum, *to think, suppose*

Q

quaero, quaerere, quaesivi or quaesii, quaesitum, *to seek, ask, inquire*
quaeso, quaesere, quaesivi and **quaesii,** *to beg, entreat*
quaestor, -oris, m., *quaestor*
quam, adv., *than, as*
quantus, -a, -um, *of what size, how great*
quare, adv., *why*
-que, conj., *and*
querella, -ae, f., *complaint*
queror, queri, questus sum, *to complain*
qui, quae, quod, rel. pron., *who, which; that*
quiesco, -ere, quievi, quietum, *to rest, repose*
quinctum (also spelled **quintum**) adv., *for the fifth time*
Quinctilis (also spelled **Quintilis**), **-is,** m., *Quintilis, the fifth month of the Roman year*
quis, quid, *who?, what?; why?*
quisquis, quidquid, *whoever, whichever, whatever*
quomodo, adv., *how, in the manner*
quondam, *once, at one time, formerly*
quoniam, conj., *since*
quoque, adv., *also, too*

R

rapio, rapere, rapui, raptum, *to seize, snatch away*
ramus, -i, m., *branch, twig*
recipio, -cipere, -cepi, -ceptum, *to receive, accept, take*
rector, -oris, m., *director, ruler*
recubo, -are, -avi, -atum, *to lie, repose*
reddo, reddere, reddidi, redditum, *to restore*
redeo, -ire, -ivi and **-ii, -itum,** *to return*
regio, -ionis, f., *region, district*
relego, -legere, -legi, -lectum, *to read again*
relinquo, -linquere, -liqui, -lictum, *to leave, leave behind, abandon, forsake*
repente, adv., *suddenly*
repurgo, -are, -avi, -atum, *to clean or clean afresh*
requiesco, requiescere, requievi, requietus, *to rest, repose*
res publica, rei publicae, f., *the republic, the state*
res, rei, f., *thing, matter, affair*
resido, -sidere, -sedi, *to settle down; of cavalry, to mount*
resisto, -sistere, -stiti, *to stop, halt*

respicio, -spicere, -spexi, -spectum, *to look back*
restituo, -uere, -ui, -utum, *to restore, replace*
revoco, -are, -avi, -atum, *to bring back*
rogo, -are, -avi, -atum, *to ask*
Romanus, -a, -um, *Roman*
roseus, -a, -um, *rose-colored*
rota, -ae, f., *wheel*
rumpo, rumpere, rupi, ruptum, *to burst open, break through*

S

sacer, sacra, sacrum, *sacred, holy, consecrated*
sacro, -are, -avi, -atum, *to dedicate*
sacrum, -i, n., *holy spot, sanctuary*
saepe, adv., *often*
saevus, -a, -um, *savage, cruel, fierce*
salus, salutis, f., *health, safety, wellbeing; greetings*
salveo, -ēre, *to be well;* (imperat.) *hello!*
Samnis, -itis, *Samnite*
sanctus, -a, -um, *sacred, holy, solemn*
sapio, -ere, -ivi and -ii, *to sense, discern*
satis, *enough*
sator, -oris, m., *sower, planter; father*
scelus, -eris, n., *wicked deed, crime; villain, criminal*
scio, scire, scivi and scii, scitum, *to know, understand*
scriptor, -oris, m., *writer*
securus, -a, -um, *untroubled, released from care, composed*
secutor, -oris, m., *secutor*
sed, conj., *but*
semper, adv., *always*
senatus, -us, m., *senate*
senex, senis, m., *old man*
sententia, -ae, f., *opinion, judgment*
sentio, sentire, sensi, sensus, *to feel, perceive*
September, -bris, m., *September,* the seventh month of the Roman year
septeni, -ae, -a, *seven at a time, seven*
septimum, adv., *for the seventh time*
sepulcrum, -i, n., *grave, tomb*
seriola, -ae, f., *jar*
sermo, sermonis, m., *speech, conversation*
servo, -are, -avi, -atum, *to keep, preserve, maintain; watch over*
sex, *six*
sextum, adv., *for the sixth time*
si, conj., *if*
sic, adv., *thus, in this way*
signum, -i, n., *sign, signal; statue*
silva, -ae, f., *forest, woods*
similis, -e, *similar to, like*
simplex, simplicis, *straightforward, frank, sincere*
simul, adv., *at the same time*
sine, prep. + abl., *without*
sinister, -tra, -trum, *left; unfavorable, adverse*
sinus, -us, m., *lap*

sisto, sistere, stiti, statum, *to stop, halt* (transitive)
situs, -a, -um, *placed, situated, located*
sol, solis, m., *sun*
solacium, -i, n., *solace, comfort*
solidus, -i, m., *solidus,* a gold coin
sollemnis, -e, *solemn, festive*
solor, -ari, -atum, *to comfort, console*
solus, -a, -um, *alone*
solvo, -ere, solvi, solutum, *loosen, release, free; scatter*
soror, sororis, f., *sister*
sors, sortis, f., *lot, fate*
spargo, -ere, sparsi, sparsum, *to scatter, sprinkle*
spatium, -i, n., *interval, span of time*
species, -ei, f., *appearance, beauty*
spero, -are, -avi, -atum, *to hope*
spes, spei, f., *hope*
statua, -ae, f., *statue*
statuo, statuere, statui, statutum, *to put up, erect*
stercus, -oris, n., *dung, manure*
sterno, -ere, stravi, stratum, *to spread out; (of a bed) to make or arrange*
stirps, stirpis, f., *stock, root, family*
studiosus, -a, -um, *eager, devoted*
studium, -i, n., *pursuit, study; enthusiasm*
sub, prep. + abl., *under*
subeo, -ire, -ii or **-ivi, -itum,** *to go under, enter; suffer*
subigo, -igere, -egi, -actum, *to subdue*
subitaneus, -a, -um, *sudden*
subito, adv., *suddenly*
succurro, -ere, -curri, -cursum, *help, run to help*
sum, esse, fui, futurum, *to be*
summus, -a, -um, *the highest*
superi, -orum, m., *gods above; humans on earth*
superstes, -stitis (+ dat.), *surviving, living beyond*
surgo, surgere, surrexi, surrectum, *to rise up*
sustineo, -tinēre, -tinui, -tentum, *hold up, bear, endure, support*
sui, sibi, se, se, *him(self), her(self), it(self), them(selves)*
suus, -a, -um, *his (own), her (own), its (own)*

T

taceo, -ēre, -ui, -itum, *be silent, say nothing*
tacitus, -a, -um, *silent, mute*
taedium, -i, n., *a nuisance, tedium*
talis, tale, *such, of such a kind*
tam, adv., *so*
tamen, conj., *however, yet, nevertheless*
tantus, -a, -um, *of such a size, so great*
tardo, -are, -avi, -atum, *to slow, delay*
tardo, -are, -avi, -atum, *to slow, delay*
tego, tegere, texi, tectum, *to cover, bury*
tempus, -oris, n., *time, span of time*
tendo, tendere, tetendi, tentum, *to strive, exert oneself*
tenebrae, -arum, f., *darkness*

teneo, tenere, tenui, tentum, *to hold*
terra, -ae, f., *earth*
tertium, adv. *for the third time*
tertius, -a, -um, *third*
testamentum, -i, n., *last will, testament*
thermae, -arum, f., *baths*
Thrax, Thracis, *Thracian*
timeo, -ēre, -ui, *to fear, be afraid of*
titulus, -i, m., *inscription*
togatus, -i, m., *Roman citizen*
tollo, tollere, sustuli, sublatum, *to lift up, raise up, take away*
torreo, torrēre, torrui, tostum, *to burn*
torus, -i, m., *couch, bed*
tot, adv., *so many*
traho, trahere, traxi, tractum, *to drag, draw, pull along*
transcurro, -currere, -cucurri, -cursum, *to run across or over; to live out*
tres, tria, *three*
tribunicius, -a, -um, *tribunician, of the tribune*
tribuo, -ere, -ui, -utum, *to confer, grant, allow*
triclinium, -i, n., *dining room*
tristis, -e, *gloomy, sullen, sad*
triumpho, -are, -avi, -atum, *to triumph, to celebrate a triumph*
tu, *you*
tumulus, -i, m., *burial mound*

U

ubi, rel. adv., *where*
ubique, *everywhere*
ullus, -a, -um, *any*
ultra, ultro, *farther, beyond, more remote*
ulula, -ae, f., *owl*
umquam, *ever*
una, adv., *together*
unde, adv., *whence, from where*
unus, -a, -um, *one*
urina, -ae, f., *urine*
uro, urere, ussi, ustum, *to burn*
usque, adv., *even*
ut, conj., *in order that, so that; as*
uterque, utraque, utrumque, *each of two, both*
unda, -ae, f., *wave*
universus, -a, -um, *whole, entire*
utilis, -e, *useful, beneficial*
utinam, adv., *would that!, oh that!*
utor, uti, usus sum (+ abl.), *to use, enjoy*

V

valeo, -ēre, -ui, -itum, *to be well; (imperat.) goodbye!*
vanus, -a, -um, *empty*
varius, -a, -um, *various*
veho, vehere, vexi, vectum, *to carry*
velox, velocis, *swift*

velum, -i, n., *sail; awning*
venatio, -onis, f., *an animal hunt*
venetus, -a, -um, *blue*
venio, venire, veni, ventum, *to come, arrive*
venter, -tris, m., *stomach, belly*
Venus, Veneris, f., the goddess *Venus*
verber, verberis, n., *rod;* (plur.) *blows, beatings*
verna, -ae, c., *house-born slave*
versiculus, -i., m., *little verse, little line*
veteranus, -a, -um, *veteran*
veto, -are, vetui, vetitum, *to forbid, prevent, outlaw*
via, -ae, f., *road, way, journey*
viator, viatoris, m., *traveler*
victor, victoris, m., *conquerer, victor*
victoria, -ae, f., *victory*
viduo, -are, -avi, -atum, *to deprive;* (pass.) *be made a widow*
vigeo, -ēre, -ui, *to thrive, flourish, be strong*
vinco, vincere, vici, victum, *to conquer, surpass, overcome*
vinc(u)lum, -i, n., *rope, chain; restraint*
vinum, -i, n., *wine*
viola, -ae, f., *violet*
violo, -are, -avi, -atum, *to violate, desecrate*
vir, viri, m., *man, husband*
viridis, -e, *green, fresh, blooming*
virtus, -tutis, f., *virtue, excellence*
viso, visere, visi, visum, *to go to see, visit*
vita, -ae, f., *life*
vitium, -i, n., *fault; defect, weakness*
vitreus, -a, -um, *glass, made of glass*
vivo, -ere, vixi, victum, *to live, be alive*
vivus, -a, -um, *alive, living*
vocito, -are, -avi, -atum, *to call, name*
volo, velle, volui, *to be willing; to wish, want*
votum, -i, n., *vow, promise*
voveo, vovēre, vovi, votus, *to dedicate, consecrate, vow*
vox, vocis, f., *voice*
vulnus, -eris, n., *wound; misfortune*

Index of Selected Grammar, Syntax, and Figures

(References are to inscription number. Boldface indicates that the inscription falls within the section targeting the selected grammar point.)

Credits for Illustrations (by inscription number)

2. Drawing by Torey Akers, from an illustration in *CIL*.
11. Drawing by Torey Akers, from an illustration in *CIL*.
16a. Photo courtesy of Helen Pope.
16b. Photo courtesy of iStockphoto ©Juergen Schnonnop.
17 Drawing by the author, from an illustration in *RIB*.
19. Drawing from a slide in the Department of Classical Languages, Phillips Exeter Academy.
27. Illustration from *Harper's Dictionary of Classical Literature and Antiquities* (New York, 1897).
33a. Illustration from *Harper's Dictionary of Classical Literature and Antiquities* (New York, 1897).
33b. Drawing from August Mau's *Pompeii, Its Life and Art* (New York, 1907), based on a Roman wall painting now housed at the Naples Archaeological Museum.
34a. Photo courtesy of Michael O'Donnell.
34b. Photo courtesy of iStockphoto ©Nikada.
44. Photo courtesy of iStockphoto ©sailorr.
55. Drawing by the author, from a photograph in *The Epigraphic Collection of the Museo Nazionale Romano at the Baths of Diocletian* (Milan, 2001).
68. Drawing by Torey Akers, from a photograph in A.E. Gordon's *Illustrated Introduction to Latin Epigraphy* (Berkeley, 1983).
88. Drawing by Torey Akers, from an illustration in *CIL*.
102. Drawing by Torey Akers, from a photograph in A.E. Gordon's *Illustrated Introduction to Latin Epigraphy* (Berkeley, 1983).
107. Photo ©The Trustees of the British Museum.
114. Photo courtesy of Helen Pope.
119. Drawing by Torey Akers, from an illustration in *CIL*.
122. Drawing by Torey Akers, from an illustration in *CIL*.
131. Photo courtesy of Michael O'Donnell.
134. Photo courtesy of the Centre for the Study of Ancient Documents, University of Oxford.
144. Photo courtesy of Michael O'Donnell.
145. Drawing by Torey Akers, from a photograph in *Pompeii A.D. 79* (New York, 1978).
154. Drawing by the author, from an illustration in *CIL*.
156. Photo ©The Trustees of the British Museum.
163a. Photo courtesy of Michael O'Donnell.
163b. Photo courtesy of Shutterstock.com.
166. Photo courtesy of Paul Langford.